The
FREE CHURCH TRADITION
in the
LIFE OF ENGLAND

THE FREE CHURCH TRADITION IN THE LIFE OF ENGLAND

by

ERNEST A. PAYNE

Senior Tutor
Regent's Park College, Oxford

SCM PRESS LTD
BLOOMSBURY STREET LONDON

TO

P.W.P.

First published September 1944
Second edition November 1944
Third edition (revised) January 1951

Printed in Great Britain by
Northumberland Press Limited
Gateshead on Tyne

Contents

Preface

EACH GENERATION must study its heritage afresh, and as the story of the past is retold, a new chapter is added and the older accounts are seen from a different standpoint, for the perspective has changed. Forty years ago, Silvester Horne's *Popular History of the Free Churches* had a great and deserved popularity, but one has only to read the preface to see what a gulf lies between his world and our own. Even Dr. Selbie's *Nonconformity* and Mr. Edward Shillito's *Hope and Mission of the Free Churches*—succinct and valuable as they are—bear clear marks of the fact that they were written before the war of 1914-18. The two substantial volumes of H. W. Clark's *The History of English Nonconformity* remain as a standard authority, but they also appeared in the years 1911-13. Moreover, they are not easily accessible, nor likely to be read by most of those I have in mind in these pages.

In what follows I have tried to recall the main outlines of the story of the Free Churches with the contemporary situation constantly before me. I have sought to make the leading personalities as vivid as severe limitations of space would allow. The references are intended to indicate where more information may be found and also to stimulate others to further study, for there are many aspects of the Free Church tradition which deserve far more attention than has been given them of recent years. It has been necessary to limit the study severely and there are, in consequence, few direct references to the situation in Scotland or to the Church of Scotland. The contribution of the Free Churches to the life of England, and through England to the world, has been my main concern. I trust that nothing I have said will give offence or seem wilfully blind to those of other branches of the Christian Church who may read these pages.

I have been much helped by the suggestions and encouragement of a number of friends, and am deeply grateful to them. Three call for special mention. Miss Joyce Booth deciphered my manuscript, and at all stages of the work gave patient and efficient assistance, without which, amid the pressure of many tasks, it could not have been completed. The Revs. J. O. Barrett and W. W. Bottoms, by the careful reading of the typescript and by their comments, have added to the debt I already owe them for many years of faithful friendship. My deepest obligations, however, for any truth or insight there may be in these pages, are, first, to a family tradition of Nonconformity stretching back to the opening of the eighteenth century and perhaps still earlier, and, secondly, to a personal experience within the Free Churches which makes me increasingly sure that they are truly a part of the one holy, catholic, apostolic Church.

E.A.P.

1944

Note to Third Edition

THIS BOOK first appeared in 1944. The second edition
was called for so speedily that only one or two minor
corrections were then possible. For this third edition, which
has been reset, the work has been carefully revised, a few
new paragraphs have been added, and the bibliographical
notes have been brought up to date. I am grateful for the
generous appreciation expressed by readers in many parts of
the world, Anglican as well as Free Church, and for the
suggestions for the improvement of the book which have
been sent to me. The six years that have passed since it
was written have brought a number of indications which
lead one to believe that the period of hesitancy chronicled
in the eighth chapter is coming to an end.

E.A.P.

CHAPTER ONE

The Churches of England

We claim more than the possession of a history.
We claim to be in and of History.

P. T. FORSYTH,
The Antiquity of Dissent, p. 5.

THE CHRISTIAN who to-day would consider a particular religious tradition, or the religious situation in a particular land, must begin by recalling the general alignment of Christians throughout the world. Almost every religious group has relationships more or less close with groups in other lands. Ecclesiastically, as well as politically, our thinking must increasingly be in global terms. Our special concern here is with the witness of the Free Churches, and in particular their history and position in the life of modern Britain. The right perspective will be gained, however, only if we first take a large view and set the Free Churches side by side with the other main traditions represented among those, now found in every continent and almost every land, who give allegiance to the Christian faith.

In its organized, institutional form Christianity falls into six main divisions: the so-called Eastern Churches, the Roman Catholic Church, the Lutheran Churches, the Reformed and Presbyterian Churches, the Anglican Church and the various Free Churches. There are, of course, a number of other communions, some going back as far as the fifth century A.D. and some of more recent origin. Within these six main divisions there are many important variations and sub-sections. The distinction between the Presbyterian and Free Churches is not in all lands easy to draw. Nevertheless, looking broadly at the Christian forces throughout the world, it is true to say that the great majority of those who claim the name belong to one or other of these groups.

History and geography have largely determined the areas where the different traditions are most strongly represented. Some lands are almost wholly of one ecclesiastical pattern and temper. In others, several different types are to be found, sometimes existing uneasily side by side. Increasingly in the last century and a half, movements of population, human contacts on an ever greater scale, and vigorous and deliberate propaganda, have led to the carrying out, from the lands of their origin to every part of the earth, of almost all these main Christian types.

The Eastern, or, as they are often called, Orthodox Churches, number in their ranks nearly all the Christians in the Balkans and the Middle East. Recent events have shown that this form of Christianity continues to have a strong hold on the Russian people, in spite of the anti-religious movements which found expression in Soviet lands after the Bolshevist Revolution. In the main, therefore, it is in a fairly compact though extensive, geographical area that the Eastern Church is dominant. The Roman communion, on the other hand, whilst it has the allegiance of almost all Christians in certain contiguous lands, is widely spread throughout the world. In Italy, France, Belgium, Spain, Portugal and the Latin countries of Central and South America, there are relatively few Christians who are not Catholics. In Germany roughly half the Christians are of this persuasion. There is an important and influential Roman Catholic community in the British Isles. There are large numbers of Catholics in America and Canada. Further, the extensive missionary activity of the Roman

Church has given it large numbers of adherents throughout Asia, Africa and Australasia. The Lutheran Churches, which owe their origin to the work of Martin Luther, are found in Germany and the Scandinavian countries. They are strongly represented in North America, and they also, through missionary activities during the last century or so, have produced sturdy daughter churches in other parts of the world. The Reformed and Presbyterian Churches, which in outlook and policy draw inspiration from John Huss and John Calvin, are strong in Czechoslovakia, Switzerland and Holland, in Scotland and Northern Ireland, in the United States, in many parts of the Netherlands Empire and the British Empire, and, as the result of missionary activity, in Africa, India and China.

Our fifth main division, the Anglican Church, is also now very widely spread throughout the world. Its familiar title, " The Church of England ", is somewhat deceptive. There it began, there it is most firmly established, there it exerts its greatest influence. It has passed out from England, however, throughout the British Empire and into all English-speaking territories. A considerable group of Christians in the United States are in communion with the Archbishop of Canterbury. The Anglican Church has gone still farther afield. Through the notable share it has taken in the recent expansion of Christianity in Africa and the East, it has now many large new missionary dioceses overseas. Of the main groups into which Christians are divided, the Anglican is far the smallest in numbers—it claims only some nine million communicants[1]—but its history and theological position have given it an importance quite out of relation to its size.

Finally, there are the Free Churches. They had their origin in Western Europe, and particularly in Britain. They were products, to begin with, of the Reformation movement,

[1] *Christian Year Book*, 1950, p. 13.

and owed much of their inspiration to Luther and Calvin, particularly the latter. They were also influenced by those who have been called " the Dissenters of the Reformation " —the Anabaptists. In the eighteenth century they were reinforced by the great Methodist movement. They had already spread to the American colonies, and through their part in the American Revolution, and in the nineteenth century opening up of the Middle and Far West, gained the religious allegiance of probably the majority of the citizens of the United States.[2] To the considerable communities in Britain and America, there have now to be added not only similar groups in different parts of the British Empire, but also the vigorous churches in Africa and the Far East, which are the product of the extensive and enthusiastic missionary activity of recent generations. There are also considerable numbers of Free Churchmen in certain European lands, and particularly in Russia. There are many differences and varieties among the Free Churches, but their history and practice, and certain common emphases they make justify our treating them together. If so treated, they clearly form a very strong and significant " bloc " in contemporary Christendom. " The broad result of the religious development of English Christianity during the last three centuries," wrote Dr. Hensley Henson, " is the indisputable fact that alike in the English-speaking communities outside Europe and in non-Christian lands, the dominant type of non-Roman Christianity is not Anglican but Dissenting."[3]

II

We turn from this cursory glance at the main ecclesiastical groupings throughout the world to consider the situation in the British Isles. It is a complex situation that confronts us.

[2] See W. L. Sperry, *Religion in America*, 1945, pp. 74f., 242.
[3] *The Church of England*, 1939, p. 249.

Four of the groups we have noted in our world survey are strongly represented. The Irish Republic is overwhelmingly Roman Catholic in its religious allegiance. Northern Ireland and Scotland are predominantly Presbyterian. Wales is mainly Nonconformist, or Free Church. England is the home of the Anglican Church, and its main stronghold, but large numbers of Christians belong to the Free Churches, and there is also a considerable Roman Catholic community. The religious situation in these islands has for the last three hundred years been anything but a simple one. Yet the variety of the religious traditions to be found in their life, and the tensions that have resulted, have undoubtedly enriched the British character. As in politics, so in religion, our people have had to work out, within the restricted limits of our territory, issues of world-wide import. Our religious history is worth the most careful study, and any great changes in our religious outlook and practice have probably implications of widespread significance for Christianity generally.

In the last forty years three main tendencies seem to have been at work in Britain. First, there has been a considerable decline in the place of organized religion in the life of the community. Secondly, there has been a notable improvement in the relations between the different groups of Christians. Thirdly, there have been some important realignments, so that the relative positions of certain of the groups have changed somewhat. On all three of these matters something must be said.

It is important not to generalize too hastily or to draw rash conclusions from the changes of a generation or so. In the long history of the Church there have been periods both of ebb and flow in religious enthusiasm. It is clear, however, that in Britain, as in Europe as a whole, recent decades have seen a general weakening of the hold of the Christian

Church on the life of the average man. Neither in the intellectual nor the practical sphere has the Church, as such, nor Christianity as a system, the authority it once had. In the nineteenth century, particularly in the second half of that century, some profession, even if only a formal one, of Christian allegiance, was almost universal. Attendance at public worship was general. Since the beginning of the twentieth century there has been a marked change. It has affected all the Christian bodies. Those which issue regular statistics have, with few exceptions, had to lament a steadily declining membership during the past twenty-five years, and an even more striking decline in the number of children under their instruction. The reasons for the change are many and various. Not all of them are bad. There was a good deal of formality and hypocrisy in much of the Christian profession of two or three generations ago. In certain spheres of life the leaders of the Christian bodies claimed and exerted an authority which did not rightly belong to them. The Christian faith has been severely tested and challenged from many different quarters. Historians, philosophers, scientists and psychologists have all submitted it to searching examination, and though their debates have lasted now for nearly a century, it is only of recent years that the bewildering effect on the mind of the common man has become apparent. At the same time the wars and revolutions of recent decades have presented a new and searching practical challenge. To some of these things we shall return later. Here we have simply to note the fact that in Britain, as in many other lands, the Christian churches have been on the defensive and have lost ground since the beginning of the century.

Secondly, there has been a marked decline in the bitterness of ecclesiastical controversy, and a notable and widespread movement towards fuller Christian unity and fellowship. The cleavage in these islands between Roman Catholics and Protestants was a very deep one. Few cries have had greater power over the average Englishman (or Scot, or Welshman) than that of " No Popery ". Moreover, the circumstances in which Free Churchmen left or were expelled from the Anglican Church, and the disabilities, civil and religious, under which they long suffered, left lingering and bitter memories. The Free Churches themselves were divided on many issues, and there was sometimes little love lost between them. Down to the end of the nineteenth century many strident and discordant notes could be heard in the discussions between the various groups of Christians, and where one or another had opportunity, there was often persecution and victimization of a petty kind. Here again, recent decades have seen a striking change. It is well illustrated by the widespread determination to avoid over the religious clauses of the Education Bill of 1944 the kind of controversy which surrounded that of 1902. The cynical outsider may be inclined to suggest that with the very foundations of the faith challenged, Christians have at last seen the necessity of moderating their internecine strife, but there is plenty of evidence that something more positive and worthy than a crude self-interest has been at work.

In 1893 the Free Churches of England formed a council for certain common purposes. Already plans were afoot for the closer union of the various Presbyterian bodies in Scotland. Soon afterwards the separated Methodist Churches began to come together. Within the Anglican Church there showed itself a deep desire for the turn of the tide which since the Reformation had caused an ever-increasing number of separate groups. The great missionary conference at Edinburgh in 1910 gave a fillip to many different movements for Christian co-operation and unity, and since the Lambeth Conference of 1920, the relationships between

B

Anglicans, Presbyterians and Free Churchmen have entered a quite new phase of cordiality and mutual recognition. Much time has been spent in negotiations regarding the possibility of church union of an organic kind. On great public occasions, such as the Coronation of King George VI and National Days of Prayer, in Westminster Abbey or in Broadcasting House, the Archbishop of Canterbury, the Moderator of the General Assembly of the Church of Scotland and leaders of the Free Churches have stood side by side, often sharing in common acts of worship, in a way that would have been quite impossible a few decades ago. Even more significant has been the fact that since 1939 there have been the beginnings of co-operation along certain lines between Anglicans and Free Churchmen on the one hand, and certain Roman Catholic organizations and individual Roman Catholics on the other. Many of these happenings will call for more extended reference later. Here we only note them as symptomatic of a new Christian cordiality, for the attitude of the leaders has been paralleled in many a city and many a village where formerly religious bigotry and suspicion prevailed.

There have been, in the third place, some important changes in the relative strength of the different religious groups in Britain. Roman Catholics have increased in numbers and influence, the Free Churches have lost ground. It is the judgment of a recent well-informed observer, Professor D. W. Brogan, that " in the generation that has passed since the great Liberal landslide of 1906, one of the greatest changes in the English religious and social landscape has been the decline of Nonconformity ".[4] At the close of the nineteenth century Englishmen were probably about equally divided numerically between the Church of England and the Free Churches. The Nonconformist leaders played a

[4] *The English People*, 1943, p. 121.

very important part not only in the religious but in the social and political life of the nation. Again it is well to remember not to judge too hastily the changes of a generation, particularly one's own, and it is necessary to keep in mind that larger world background to which allusion has already been made. Here, also, more detailed consideration will be given to the causes at work. Nevertheless, it is obvious that the Free Churches have lost a good deal of the enthusiasm and vigour that characterized them in the second half of the nineteenth century. They are no longer so sure of themselves. The observer just quoted suggests that the decline of Nonconformity has been partly due to " the comparative irrelevance of the peculiarly Nonconformist (as apart from Christian) view of the contemporary world and its problems ".[5] This is a serious charge. It invites a re-examination of the history and witness of the Free Churches and a consideration of their present position and future prospects.

III

There can be no doubt at all as to the importance of the Free Church contribution to the making of modern England. There are those who try to ignore it. Some who write of the development of the religious life of this country treat Nonconformity as relatively insignificant, deserving only a few pages or an appendix. Not a few who try to describe Britain and her people, and to understand her tradition, see the parish church but overlook the Nonconformist chapel. As a result they give a very distorted picture and fail rightly to understand our national characteristics. We are what we are because Free Churches have played so big a part in our life.

The Free Churches are as " English " as the Church of England herself. There is justice in the claim, made by a

[5] *The English People,* 1943, p. 121.

shrewd observer, that " they represent in this land, perhaps, the most distinctive product of the Christian Faith in its work upon the national character ".[6] Their very variety may be taken as confirmation of this. Their influence has been felt on many different sides of our life. How much of our national story is connected with the names of Cromwell and Milton, Fox and Bunyan, Watts and Doddridge, the Wesleys and Whitefield, William Carey and David Livingstone, C. H. Spurgeon and R. W. Dale, John Bright and Joseph Chamberlain, Hugh Price Hughes and John Clifford, Joseph Arch and Keir Hardie—all of them men shaped and moulded by their associations with the Free Churches. When most deeply stirred, the Englishman instinctively expresses his religious emotion in hymns written by Nonconformists. " Our God, our help in ages past ", " Jesus shall reign where'er the sun ", " O God of Bethel ", " Before Jehovah's awful throne ": these, and the hymns of Charles Wesley, have become an integral part of our English tradition. Take away the Nonconformist contribution to civil and religious liberty, to the ending of the slave-trade and the emancipation of the slaves, to popular education, to social progress and philanthropy, and many of the most glorious and stirring pages in our national record disappear. Many of those most respected in our public life, even of recent days, are the children of Free Church homes, and have owed much of their character and authority to their Free Church inheritance. Most important of all in the past has been the influence of the Nonconformist outlook and temper on the average British citizen.

Historians and those students best qualified to judge are increasingly recognizing the importance of the Free Church contribution to our national tradition. In 1912, M. Elie

[6] E. Shillito, *The Hope and Mission of the Free Churches*, 1912, p. 10. Cf. G. Kitson Clark, *The English Inheritance*, 1950.

Halévy, the distinguished French historian, published the first volume of a very important and significant study of our recent British history and culture.[7] Marked by impartiality and discrimination, it emphasizes in a very striking way the influence of evangelical Christianity on modern England and the part played by the " dissenting sects " in our national life. M. Halévy begins by focusing his attention upon the year 1815, though he moves both backwards and forwards from that date, and it is the Methodist movement that impresses him most, though he shows keen appreciation of the contribution of the older Nonconformist bodies. Methodism is, in his opinion, the explanation of " the extra-ordinary stability which English Society was destined to enjoy throughout a period of revolution and crises; what we may truly term the miracle of modern England, anarchist but orderly, practical and businesslike, but religious and even pietist ".[8]

Sir Ernest Barker in a courageous lecture he delivered in Hamburg in 1936 on " Oliver Cromwell and the English People "—a lecture aimed at replying to the parallels then being drawn in Germany between Cromwell and Hitler—described the Protector as " the incarnation—perhaps the greatest we have had—of the genius of English Noncon-formity, which is the peculiar and (it may even be said) the cardinal factor in the general development of English politics and English national life ".[9] More recently, in his important and attractive study *Britain and the British People*, Sir Ernest Barker has urged that religion is the key to the under-

---

[7] Vol. I, 1912 (English translation, 1924); Vols. II and III, 1923; Vol. IV, 1926; Vol. V, 1932. The last forms an Epilogue dealing with the years 1895-1905. M. Halévy's death in 1937 left the period from 1841-95 uncovered. *The Age of Peel and Cobden, 1841-52*, has now appeared posthumously.

[8] Introduction to Book III.

[9] *Oliver Cromwell*, Cambridge Miscellany, 1937, p. 28. Cf. pp. 61-2.

standing of the development of English life, and that it was the struggle and tension between Anglicans and Tories on the one side, and Free Churchmen and Whigs on the other, from the end of the seventeenth to the middle of the nineteenth century, which explains our national development. "National divisions and the issues of national debate have been mainly religious; and social and political issues have arisen within a religious framework and displayed themselves in a religious setting."[10] The divisions of confessions proved, he thinks, a valuable anti-toxin against the divisions of classes. And to the attitude and temper of Nonconformity he ascribes our British conception of religious liberty, our doctrine of the limited State—a State based on free association and proceeding by free discussion—our general temper of individual self-reliance.

The connection between Nonconformity and modern democracy has received special attention of recent years. The great work of Ernst Troeltsch, *Die Soziallehren der Christlichen Kirchen und Gruppen*,[11] published in 1911, stressed the importance of the contribution to political and social thinking of the more radical Reformation groups both on the Continent and in England. "Democracy," says Dr. A. D. Lindsay, writing under the influence of Troeltsch and before the outbreak of the 1939-45 war, "is the application to social life of the principle of the spiritual priesthood of all believers. . . . If there cannot be free Churches except in a free State, there cannot be a free State unless there is

[10] *Op. cit.*, p. 94. Cf. pp. 23-6 and Ch. V. *passim*. Cf. G. M. Trevelyan, *An Autobiography*, 1949, p. 197 : " From the Restoration to the latter years of the nineteenth century, the continuity of the two parties in English politics was very largely due to the two-party system in religious observance, popularly known as Church and Chapel."
[11] E. Troeltsch, *The Social Teaching of the Christian Churches*, 1931.

in it a free Church."[12] More recently he has put it thus: "The democratic State is at best only an analogy of the really democratic religious congregation."[13] He regards the influence of the so-called "Puritans of the Left", both in this country and in America, as decisive in the development and essential for the maintenance of our democratic way of life. A number of other writers might be cited. In the works of J. L. and B. Hammond and of Professor G. D. H. Cole will be found ample acknowledgment of the part played by Nonconformists in the early struggles of the working man for political and social enfranchisement. Dr. Reinhold Niebuhr, of America, may also be noted as one who has drawn attention in his Gifford Lectures,[14] and elsewhere, to the substantial contributions to the spirit of liberty and toleration of sectarian Protestantism. He traces also a connection between Gerrard Winstanley, the leader of the Diggers in Cromwellian times, and modern communism.

IV

If, therefore, Professor Brogan is right in suggesting that the peculiarly Nonconformist outlook has become, or is becoming, irrelevant in the modern world, then an end has come to a very rich and fruitful movement in English history and in Christian history, and its demise should be worthily celebrated with the hope that the positive values for which it has stood may live on in some new form. But is he right? Is not the decline in Nonconformity something not only regrettable but also dangerous? Are not many of our present ills due to the loss of vigour among the Free Churches? Is not Professor Brogan's own comment worth

[12] *The Church and Democracy*, 1934, pp. 31 and 74.
[13] *Religion, Science and Society in the Modern World*, 1943, p. 19.
[14] *The Nature and Destiny of Man*, Vol. I, 1941; Vol. II, 1943. Cf. W. Haller, *The Rise of Puritanism*, 1938, p. 177.

pondering: "It is not evident that the Birmingham of Mr. Neville Chamberlain and the Federation of British Industries is in this respect (i.e. of the Nonconformist conscience with the sense of duty and of social obligation it inspired) an improvement on the Birmingham of Dr. Dale and John Bright."[15] Is not Professor Brogan also right in hinting that the loss of power of the Free Churches, with all that it implies, is a complicating factor in British and American relations? Further, are not many of the least satisfactory features of the political and religious situation on the Continent largely explained by the fact that the Left Wing of the Reformation movement was there successfully suppressed?[16] And are not the strength of the Free Church movement throughout the world, and its important strategic position, things that should make us pause before we readily acquiesce in its decline in this country?

These questions ought to be faced. They should be considered by those adhering to other Christian traditions. They should be remembered by those who, of recent years, have turned from the rock whence they were hewn and the hole of the pit whence they were digged. They should be the urgent concern of Free Churchmen themselves. Have the Free Churches still a mission and message, or is their day over? Have they served their purpose and should they cease their witness? Is there a place for them in post-war England and amid modern realignments, theological and ecclesiastical?

Before attempting an answer, it will be necessary to refresh our memories regarding the story of the Free Churches

[15] *The English People*, p. 130.
[16] Cf. Forsyth, *Faith, Freedom and the Future*, 1912, p. 41: "Germany has never got over the Reformers' *dragonnade* of the Anabaptists any more than France has got over the Bartholomew." This was said nearly forty years ago. The modern history of both Germany and France has emphasized its truth.

from the seventeenth century down to our own day. The important developments of the nineteenth century are only just falling into perspective. The story, in any case, needs retelling in each generation, and not only are there many to-day who have forgotten it, there are also many, even within the Free Churches, who have never heard it. For there has been in many quarters an impatience of religious divisions, understandable though not without its dangers. There has been also a real sense of bewilderment, due in part to the shattering experiences of two world wars and vast social upheavals, and due in part to the drawing together of the various Christian traditions to which allusion has already been made. Improved relationships and discussions about organic union between groups which have long been separate have given to some the impression that differences of emphasis and polity matter little or nothing. Knowledge of the past is a useful antidote to such an attitude.

What M. Halévy and Professor E. H. Carr say of England during the past few decades applies with particular force to the Free Churches in England. There has been a decline in assurance and self-confidence. Professor Carr urges that the marked revival of British unity, initiative and determination after 1940 is ground for hope that the country will retain and further strengthen that sense of mission without which she will surely decay.[17] It is probably worthy of note that the years of increasing national uncertainty and self-distrust were the years of what Professor Brogan calls "the decline of Nonconformity". It is in any case certain that without a renewed sense of mission, without a renewal of their spiritual convictions, the Free Churches of England are certain to suffer further weakening. What, then, is it that they have said and suffered for? Is it still needed?

[17] *Conditions of Peace*, 1942, pp. 130 and 186.

CHAPTER TWO

Protest: The Beginnings of Free Church Witness

The essential meaning of the Free Church system . . .
is the destruction of the medieval and early Protestant
idea of a social order welded together by one uniform
State Church, and of one infallible authority with a
uniform control of the whole of civilization.

E. TROELTSCH,
*The Social Teaching of the
Christian Churches*, p. 656.

ORIGINS ARE elusive things, and the decision as to
where to begin a story must always be somewhat arbi-
trary. When and where did the English Free Churches
have their origin? Their nineteenth-century historian,
Skeats, claimed that John Hooper, Bishop of Gloucester in
the reign of Edward VI, was the first Nonconformist. " It
was Hooper's voice," he says, " that first publicly proclaimed
the principles of religious freedom. He stood alone among
English Protestants of his age in denying the right of the
State to interfere with religion."[1] Skeats was followed by
W. F. Adeney, who wrote: " The origin of Nonconformity
may be traced back to the first Act of Uniformity in English
history "[2] (that is, that by which Edward VI, in 1549, sought

[1] Skeats & Miall, *History of the Free Churches of England*, 1891
edition, p. 7.
[2] *Encyclopedia of Religion and Ethics*, IX, p. 383, article " Nonconformity ".

to enforce the use of the first English Prayer Book). But though Hooper was a man worthy of honour for his staunch Protestantism, and his sincere religious zeal, his chief quarrel with the authorities during the reign of Edward VI seems to have been over vestments. He supported the accession of Mary to the throne, but in 1555 was burnt in Gloucester for his refusal to return to the Roman Church, in which he had been brought up. It is among the Protestant congregations of Mary's reign that Professor William Haller, one of the outstanding modern authorities on Puritanism, finds the seeds of historic English dissent.[3]

R. W. Dale claims that " the first regularly constituted English Congregational Church of which any record or tradition remains was the Church of which Richard Fitz was pastor ".[4] This he identifies with a group arrested at Plumber's Hall, London, on June 19th, 1567, at a gathering falsely claimed to be a wedding, but in reality a meeting for worship held in defiance of Elizabeth's Act of Uniformity. Champlin Burrage, after the most careful research,[5] rejects the identification made by Dale. The Plumber's Hall company were Puritans in his view, but not Separatists, concerned, that is, for the purity of the National Church, but not desirous of separating from it, whilst the group of which Fitz was pastor, though certainly a separatist congregation, with an important place in the evolution of real congregational church polity, did not seek to be a group permanently separate from the national church. Fitz's company were hostile to Roman Catholicism and wanted the Queen and her ministers to amend their religious settlement in a more radical direction.

[3] *The Rise of Puritanism,* 1938, p. 176.
[4] *History of English Congregationalism*, 1907, p. 95.
[5] *Early English Dissenters*, 1912, Ch. II. Cf. Scott Pearson, *Thomas Cartwright*, 1925, pp. 79f.

It is to Robert Browne that Champlin Burrage would look as the real pioneer of English Congregationalism, and, as Troeltsch observes, " the historical starting-point of the Free Churches . . . (lies) . . . in Congregationalism ".[6] It was in 1580 or 1581 that Browne gathered a little company together at Norwich and led them " to join themselves to the Lord in one covenant and fellowship together, and to keep and seek agreement under His laws and government ", with Browne himself, then a young man of about thirty, as their pastor. They were set upon " reformation without tarying for anie "—to use one of his most notable phrases—and their leader was destined to give his name to a movement and a party, and to have a decisive share in Free Church beginnings. It is his life and work that are generally taken to mark the deliberate establishment of groups claiming to be full and true Christian churches, yet separate from the Church of England, and rejecting the authority of Pope, bishops and State.

Whether we start with John Hooper and 1549, or with Richard Fitz and 1567, or with Robert Browne and 1581, matters relatively little. Free Church origins carry us back to Reformation times and to the stormy but exhilarating transition period between the medieval and the modern world. The year 1559 is taken by Professor G. M. Trevelyan to be the birth-year both of modern England and modern Scotland, and it is the Elizabethan religious settlement (which was rejected by the separatists) and the work of John Knox (which established Presbyterianism in Scotland), which he sees as the foundations of the new era in secular as well as religious affairs.[7] The Free Churches were born, that is to say, in one of the great creative periods of English

[6] *Social Teaching*, p. 661.   Cf. Peel, *The First Congregational Churches*, 1920.
[7] *History of England,* pp. 330f.

history. They came out of the England which produced Drake and Raleigh, Edmund Spenser and Sir Philip Sidney, Christopher Marlowe and William Byrd, the England of Shakespeare.

II

We cannot, however, confine our attention to the English scene. The period had a larger significance, and what happened in Britain can be understood only if it is given a wider setting. For several generations, indeed for two centuries, there had been signs of ferment throughout Western Europe. It was a ferment in the social, political, intellectual and religious spheres. That in the religious sphere was the most important, for throughout the Middle Ages the Church had controlled and directed all sides of life. The Pope had assumed supreme authority throughout Christendom. Canon Law was the basis of society. The elaborate system of medieval Catholicism, its forms and ceremonies, its orders and hierarchy, controlled all human activities. From time to time, in different parts of Western Europe, rebels and heretics raised their voices, but they were most of them swiftly and effectively suppressed. The Church had preserved much of the heritage of the ancient world when, in the fifth and sixth centuries, the wild barbarian peoples of Central and South-eastern Europe overran the frontiers of the Roman Empire. She had been the agent and guardian of civilization and culture for nearly a thousand years, but she was growing old and set in her ways, corrupt, ruled by vested interests, the home of privilege and power rather than of life and spiritual renewal. The price to be paid for the centralized authority, the order, the unity, which the Church gave, rose higher and higher.

One of the most notable and portentous of the protests against the Papal system came from the Englishman, John

Wyclif, in the fourteenth century. Silvester Horne, H. W. Clark and other Free Church historians[8] begin their accounts with his life and work. He is indeed of great significance, for he appealed directly to Scripture; he translated the Bible into the English vernacular, turning aside increasingly in his later years from Latin, the language of Church and State, to that of the common people; he rejected the accepted teaching about the change in the bread and wine at the Communion Service, questioning the philosophy which underlay its formulation; his " evangelical men ", or " poor priests ", were sent out preaching through the country-side, proclaiming the gospel and showing sympathy with the wrongs, sufferings and hopes of the downtrodden peasantry. " On some sides in the daring of his concepts," says H. B. Workman, " he is a Nonconformist of Nonconformists, a Modernist of the Moderns."[9]   Nevertheless, Workman agrees that in the main Wyclif is a medievalist. Bernard Manning, in a more recent study, describes him as " the conscience of his own generation ".[10] Yet in two important directions he prepared the way for subsequent developments. The influence of the Lollards on the national life and character was probably deeper than is sometimes supposed. Their traditions prepared men for the teaching of Anabaptist refugees and that of the Separatists and Nonconformists.[11] Secondly, Wyclif's ideas found a lodging on the

[8] S. Horne, *Popular History of the Free Churches*, 1903. H. W. Clark, *History of English Nonconformity,* 1911, I, pp. 23f. Cf. W. B. Selbie, *Nonconformity*, 1912. R. W. Dale, *op. cit.*, begins with a rapid review of the history of the Church from apostolic times, tracing in Montanism, Novatianism, Donatism, the free religious communities of the Middle Ages, the Waldenses, etc., certain principles analogous to those later asserted by Congregationalism.

[9] *John Wyclif*, Oxford University Press, 1926, I, p. 7.

[10] *Cambridge Medieval History*, Vol. VII, 1932, p. 506.

[11] Cf. J. Gairdner, *Lollardy and the Reformation in England*, 1908, G. M. Trevelyan, *England in the Age of Wyclif*, 1899, Ch. IX, and Gordon Rupp, *The English Protestant Tradition*, 1947, Ch. I.

Continent by way of John Huss, of Prague, who was burnt as a heretic in 1415 by order of the Council of Constance, which also directed that Wyclif's body should be disinterred and burned. The followers of Huss were divided and distracted, and Bohemia was not in the main stream of the life of the Continent. Nevertheless, the questions raised by Wyclif and Huss contributed to the louder and more effective challenges which were soon to be heard.

The fifteenth century was one of the most significant in European history. It began with the burning of Huss. It saw the discoveries of the great voyagers, which set all life in an immensely widened geographical perspective. The revived study of Greek language and literature started the Renaissance on its course. The invention of printing from movable type revolutionized education and learning. Nationalism began to show itself as a force disruptive of the ecclesiastical unity of Western Europe. The rigid structure of medieval Catholicism proved unable to adapt itself quickly enough to changing conditions; its corruptions and abuses were seen more and more clearly. The situation wanted but a man big and brave enough to utter the emancipating word. In 1483 Martin Luther was born.

The year 1517, when Luther nailed his protests on the door of the church in Wittenberg, is usually taken as the beginning of the Reformation, the most significant and far-reaching event in Christian history since the conversion of the Roman Empire. The repercussions of Luther's challenge were felt in ever-widening circles. The new spiritual life which burst forth was soon flowing in a number of different channels. Lutheran churches carried on the tradition of Luther himself. Reformed churches followed the teaching of his younger contemporary, the Frenchman, John

Calvin. Yet others favoured the views of the Swiss, Zwingli. The Roman Church itself received a new spiritual impulse through what is now called the Counter-Reformation, a movement associated with the Council of Trent and with Loyola, Xavier and others. As the struggles and controversies developed, political and social factors played an ever more important part. Motives became more and more mixed. Some reformers were increasingly ready to compromise; others put forward views ever more radical and revolutionary. Church life, as organized by Calvin, was to be as influential as his theology. The later Free Churches were deeply indebted to all sides of Calvinism. The judgment of a distinguished historian is therefore of note. " Calvin gave to his Reformed Church," says Ramsay Muir, " a form of government more democratic than anything, lay or ecclesiastical, that had yet been seen in the modern world. Each congregation, each district, each national church, was to be controlled by an elected body, including laymen as well as clerics. . . . What contribution had the Reformation made to the civilization and to the liberties of Europe? It had shattered beyond repair the unity of Christendom. In the name of religion, it had brought into Europe ' not peace, but a sword '. But it had raised the banner of freedom of belief, however much this might be obscured by the compromises and dogmatisms of the Reformers. And, in its Calvinist form, it had created a democratic system which was later to have profound effects in the political sphere."[12]

Meantime, the Anabaptists, or " re-baptizers ", had appeared on the left wing of the Reformation movement. They were among those whom Troeltsch calls " the stepchildren of the Reformation ". They found no warrant in

[12] *Civilization and Liberty*, 1940, p. 91.

Scripture for the baptism of infants, and from 1525 onwards began to form separate groups. Hubmaier and Denck[13] were two of their outstanding leaders, and, though fiercely persecuted by both Romans and Lutherans, the movement quickly spread, particularly in the still Catholic parts of the Empire and among the lower classes. "The Anabaptist ideal," it has been said, " implied a self-governing congregation, independent of state or episcopal control, having the Bible as its law, and living a rather ascetic life of strict conformity to a literal interpretation of supposedly Biblical requirements."[14] To these things were joined apocalyptic hopes. The older reformers quickly took fright at such radicalism, and the Anabaptist name was brought into enduring disrepute by tragic and disgraceful happenings in Münster between 1533 and 1535—where community of wives as well as possessions was forcibly established, while the city resisted siege by the bishop. The result was the harsh suppression of the movement. However, not a few of those who fled from England during the persecution of Protestants by Mary and of Puritans by Elizabeth had contact with Anabaptists, as they did with Lutherans and Calvinists. In the second half of the sixteenth century there were isolated Anabaptists, chiefly foreigners, in England. Much of the best of the Anabaptist tradition passed in the Netherlands into Mennonite churches, and it was with these

---

[13] H. C. Vedder, *Balthasar Hubmaier*, 1905. Alfred Coutts, *Hans Denck*, 1927. In his *Spiritual Reformers of the Sixteenth and Seventeenth Centuries*, 1914, Rufus Jones seeks to remove Denck from the ranks of the Anabaptists and to treat him as " the earliest exponent in the sixteenth century of a fresh and unique type of religion ", that of the " Inward Word " (*op. cit.*, Ch. II).

[14] Williston Walker, *A History of the Christian Church*, 1928, p. 368. On the Anabaptist movement generally, see Rufus Jones, *Studies in Mystical Religion*, 1909, Chs. XVI and XVII, R. J. Smithson, *The Anabaptists*, 1935, and E. A. Payne, *The Anabaptists of the Sixteenth Century*, 1949.

churches that many of the earliest English Separatists had contact during their exile.

The source, therefore, of the English Free Churches cannot be sought in any one place. Their antecedents were many and various. Wyclif as well as Luther, Huss as well as Calvin, Hubmaier as well as Menno Simons contributed consciously or unconsciously, directly or indirectly, to the stand taken by Robert Browne and his friends, even though it was finally independent study of the Bible and Elizabeth's determination to secure national uniformity, both religiously and politically, that caused the Puritan and Separatist movements to develop as they did.

III

Something more must be said as to what was at work in men's minds and hearts in this period of upheaval and controversy. The discoveries and inventions of the fifteenth century opened up new and bewildering worlds and brought with them new spiritual needs. These the Church, in its traditional form, did not satisfy. Indeed, it was exploiting those under its authority. It had become a great worldly institution, and increasingly the more sincere and sensitive felt thwarted and frustrated. Religiously, intellectually and politically the Papacy tried to repress the growingly restive spirit of the age. But men could not be kept under control by an institution as corrupt as the medieval Church had become, nor by the methods it was ready to employ. The deepest need was in the realm of personal religion, and though many other factors were at work and played their part in the subsequent struggles, the Reformation was primarily and genuinely a religious movement, and the crisis which precipitated it a theological crisis. We are, perhaps, better able to understand this at the present time than for several generations.

Great as had been the achievement of the medieval Church, great as had been its services to civilization, it failed men in their hour of need. The corruption surrounding the Papal Curia had become glaring and notorious. The burning words of Luther in his "Address to the Christian Nobility of the German Nation respecting the Reformation of the Christian Estate" (1520) were not too strong, and their truth was implicitly, if not explicitly, recognized by what was done at the Council of Trent (1545-63). "There is," said Luther, in his trenchant denunciation of the Papacy, "a buying and a selling, a changing, blustering and bargaining, cheating and lying, robbing and stealing, debauchery and villainy, and all kinds of contempt of God, that Antichrist himself could not rule worse. . . . Here vows are annulled; here a monk obtains leave to quit his order; here priests can enter married life for money; here bastards can become legitimate; and dishonour and shame may arrive at high honour; all evil report and disgrace is knighted and ennobled."[15] The Church as a whole may not have been as degenerate as Luther came to think. There were tragic losses as well as gains as a result of the Reformation struggle. But Luther's indictment of the abuses he saw around him could not be gainsaid.

There was among Luther and his associates a violent reaction from the system which tolerated such things. Protestantism has been defined as the revolt of genuine religion against secularization.[16] The early Separatists and the founders of the Free Churches stood in the Protestant succession, and to understand their aims and outlook, it has to be borne in mind that they inherited certain things from

[15] Wace & Buchheim, *Luther's Primary Works*, 1896, p. 187.
[16] Inge, *Protestantism*, 1931 edition, p. 9. On the Reformation movement generally see Charles Beard, *The Reformation of the Sixteenth Century*, Hibbert Lectures, 1883, and T. M. Lindsay, *History of the Reformation*, 2 vols., 1906.

the earlier generations of the Reformation movement. From Luther himself they had learned the great doctrine of justification by faith; from the Reformers generally they had learned to appeal to Scripture and to base themselves on careful study of its text. From Calvin they gained the belief that they were to be " fellow-workers with a transcendent God, not in the mystical sense . . . but as soldiers in an army on the side of God against the powers of evil ";[17] in his great *Institutes* (1536) they read the fullest and ablest exposition of the Protestant position, and in his citadel, Geneva, they many of them found a city of refuge when they were persecuted. From Zwingli and the Anabaptists came other elements in their inheritance. The former was a scholar and a Humanist, brought up in republican Switzerland and therefore with strong democratic sympathies. The Anabaptists gave them further encouragement to new experiments based upon a study of the New Testament, and in particular contributed to their inquiry as to the real nature of the Church. These summary statements may serve to indicate the richness and strength of the impulses coming from the main sections of the Continental Reformation.

" The one definite thing which can be said about the Reformation in England is that it was an act of State."[18] These words have the weighty authority of Professor F. M. Powicke behind them, and they are, of course, true. The political and personal issue of Henry VIII's marriage caused the break between England and Rome. The swaying fortunes of the subsequent struggle were largely determined by the outlook of the succeeding occupants of the throne, first Edward VI, then Mary, then Elizabeth. There was less

[17] Inge, *op. cit.*, p. 61. Cf. C. H. Garrett, *The Marian Exiles*, 1938, M. M. Knappen, *Tudor Puritanism*, Chicago, 1939, and A. Dakin, *Calvinism*, 1940.

[18] *The Reformation in England*, 1941, p. 1. Cf. G. M. Trevelyan, *History of England*, 1926, p. 329.

fanaticism, less cruelty, more compromise, than prevailed on the Continent. Reasons of public policy played a large part in the final decision that this should be a Protestant and not a Catholic land. Spain was Catholic, and Spain was our enemy. Though all this is true, however, it would be a great mistake to ignore the underlying religious needs and motives which were not essentially dissimilar from those at work in Europe generally. In England there had been grave ecclesiastical abuses. Here, as on the Continent, the reaction showed itself not only in a breaking away from the authority of the Pope, but also in a wave of anti-clericalism. Here also men discovered with a sense of relief and wonder that they could have direct access to God, and that peace of heart came by faith, not by works. Coverdale and Tyndale made effective the dream of Wyclif, so that " by the end of Elizabeth's reign, the book of books for Englishmen was the Bible ".[19] Here also, with eager enthusiasm, men set themselves to restore the discipline and practice of the primitive Church, and were led on step by step to an examination of its very foundations. The policy of Elizabeth established the Church of England with the monarch as its head and in intimate relation to the State, with episcopal government, and with the Prayer Book and Thirty-nine Articles as its formularies.

It was largely because this religious settlement was a compromise astutely conceived and rigorously enforced, that the Puritan party remained dissatisfied with it, but it was their consciences and not their political interests that dictated their opposition. What began as disputes over secondary matters, vestments, ceremonial, etc., became increasingly controversies over order, discipline and doctrine.[20] Thomas Cart-

[19] Trevelyan, *History of England*, p. 367. Cf. J. F. Mozley, *William Tyndale*, 1937.
[20] See *Puritan Manifestoes* (edited by Frere and Douglas), 1907, and the Minute Book of the Dedham " Classis " or Conference, 1582-89 (edited by R. G. Usher, Camden Society, 1905).

wright, who for a short time held the Lady Margaret Chair of Divinity in Cambridge, marks an important transition. He did not meddle with the vestiarian controversy, says his biographer. "He dealt with a matter that was to turn Puritanism into a new channel, the question of the ministry and ecclesiastical government. No matter how innocent his intentions, his lectures marked a new point of departure in the history of Puritanism and both parties were conscious of the change."[21] Since the State took the line it did, men were driven gradually to question and challenge the whole conception of the State-Church relation, till in the end there came out of Puritanism, Separatism with its doctrine of " the gathered church ", its appeal to the open Bible and the guidance of the Spirit, its demand for religious toleration.

IV

These processes can be seen at work in the story of the Separatist pioneers. They represented but a small and troublesome minority in the exciting days of Elizabeth, but they bore a heroic and costly witness, and they prepared the way for developments of profound significance in the national life and in the history of the Christian Church. They were, most of them, able and educated men, not a few of them wealthy and well connected. Browne, Barrow, Greenwood, Penry and Smyth had all been at Cambridge University. Helwys was a student at Gray's Inn.[22] They were led on step by step to an ever more radical challenging

[21] Scott Pearson, *Thomas Cartwright and Elizabethan Puritanism*, 1925, p. 33.
[22] See F. J. Powicke, *Robert Browne, Pioneer of Modern Congregationalism*, 1910, and W. H. Burgess, *John Smith the Se-Baptist*, 1911. *The Works of John Smyth* were edited for the Cambridge University Press by W. T. Whitley in 1915. J. H. Shakespeare, *Baptist and Congregational Pioneers*, 1906, gives sketches of Browne, Barrow, Greenwood, Penry, Johnson, Smyth, Robinson and Jacob. The

of the religious policy of the Queen and her Archbishop, both of whom tried to enforce uniformity of doctrine and discipline throughout the realm with all the resources at their command. They were aided by spies and a secret police, and by a strict censorship of all publications. Sincere religious convictions could thus easily be made to appear as treason, even though the charge of disloyalty was vigorously repudiated by the victims. The struggles of Christian leaders against Nazism in Germany and in occupied Norway, reproduced in many respects what happened in Elizabethan England.

Robert Browne was born about 1550 near Stamford. He could claim connection with Elizabeth's great minister, William Cecil, Lord Burghley, and was educated at Cambridge in the days when Thomas Cartwright was criticizing the policy of the Church of England from a Puritan standpoint, and criticizing it so trenchantly that he lost his chair and had to seek refuge on the Continent. Young Browne entered the priesthood full of zeal and eagerness, but during a visit to Holland, helped probably by contact with Dutch Anabaptists, he became convinced that only by complete separation from the State could the Church properly order its affairs according to the mind of Christ. As we have seen, he gathered a little company together in 1580-1 at Norwich. Within a few months the attentions of the authorities compelled them to seek refuge in Middelburg, to which there shortly afterward migrated the Merchant Adventurers' Church, which was Presbyterian in polity and had Cart-

second of these is treated at greater length in F. J. Powicke, *Henry Barrow and the Exiled Church of Amsterdam*, 1900. For Penry see William Pierce, *John Penry*, 1923, and *The Notebook of John Penry* (edited by Albert Peel, Camden Series, 1944). *The Mistery of Iniquity* by Thomas Helwys was reproduced by Replika process in 1935, with an introduction by H. Wheeler Robinson. On the Marprelate Tracts see William Pierce, *An Historical Introduction to the Marprelate Tracts*, 1908.

wright as its minister. A few years later, for reasons that will probably always remain a mystery, Browne changed his views, submitted to the demands of the authorities and spent the last four decades of his long life as rector of Achurch, in Northamptonshire. But the work of his youth, and in particular his challenging writings, started a movement which could not be stayed. The mantle of Browne passed to John Greenwood, a Cambridge man some ten years his junior, who, after a period as a clergyman with strong Puritan sympathies, adopted Separatist views and joined himself to a group of about a hundred persons meeting secretly in London for worship and Bible study. Greenwood influenced Henry Barrow, a fiery son of Norfolk, converted after a rather dissolute youth, and Barrow who, like Browne, had family connections with Burghley, was soon the leader of the London company.

Archbishop Whitgift turned his attention to them in 1586. Greenwood was arrested with others, and Barrow lost his liberty because he returned to London to see his friend, and carelessly started an argument as to what the title " bishop " means in the New Testament. The five examinations of Greenwood and Barrow show them contending bravely and acutely against all threats and brow-beatings for the claim that " Christ is only head of His Church and His laws may no man alter ". After several years of imprisonment under shocking conditions, in April, 1593, the two friends were hanged at Tyburn. Even Lord Burghley thought that Whitgift was going a little too far in his severity.

A few months before, the London Separatists, now formed in orderly fashion into a church, had been joined by an ardent Welshman, then in his early thirties—John Penry. Penry had been both at Cambridge and Oxford. He had become an eager Puritan and, though he had not sought ordination, engaged in widespread open-air preaching in his

native land. He probably had an important share in the
writing and issuing of the provocative Marprelate Tracts,
which came from a secret press, and which attacked the
bishops " in a railing rollicking style " from the Presbyterian
standpoint. The preaching of the gospel was his main concern, but when Whitgift and the authorities got hold of him
they swiftly compassed his end. He was hanged in May, 1593.
He bequeathed a Bible to each of his four small daughters,
and ended his will thus: " I leave the success of my labours,
the calling of my country to the knowledge of Christ's
blessed Gospel, unto such of my countrymen as the Lord
is to raise after me."   Penry is said to have been the
first to advise Puritans and Nonconformists to emigrate
to the American colonies in the hope of finding freedom
there.

Browne, Greenwood, Barrow and Penry were the pioneers
of Congregationalism. On the question of baptism they
were somewhat hesitant and perplexed.[23] But this issue
had to be faced. It was raised by John Smyth, also a Cambridge man, but twenty years younger than Browne and
Greenwood. After a time as an Anglican clergyman, he
joined himself about 1606 to the Separatist Church at Gainsborough, bringing with him his friend, Thomas Helwys, a
well-connected Nottinghamshire gentleman. Smyth became
pastor of the Gainsborough company who had " as the
Lord's free people joined themselves, by a covenant of the
Lord, into a Church Estate in the fellowship of the Gospel
to walk in all His ways made known, or to be made known,
according to their best endeavours whatsoever it should cost
them ".[24] When it was clear that the régime of James I was
going to give no more liberty than that of his predecessor,

[23] See, e.g., F. J. Powicke, *Henry Barrow*, pp. 110-14.
[24] The words are William Bradford's. See W. H. Burgess, *op. cit.*,
p. 84.

Smyth and Helwys effected the migration of the members from Lincolnshire to Amsterdam, whither most of the London Separatists had already preceded them. Smyth was a frail, dauntless man of majestic personality, a spiritual pioneer gradually making his way towards the truth as he could discern it. In 1609, in Amsterdam, he came to the conclusion that infant baptism was no baptism at all in the New Testament sense, but that baptism was commanded by Christ, and was the basis of church fellowship. He therefore baptized himself, then his friend Helwys, and afterwards such of the Amsterdam company as were ready to unite with him. Thus there came into existence the first (English) Baptist church. Smyth, however, came to have doubts as to the rightness of his action in baptizing himself and turned towards the Mennonites as the true Church.

Helwys could no longer follow his friend, and some months before Smyth's death in 1612, he and about a dozen others felt it their duty to return to London, in spite of the danger, and bear their witness there. In Spitalfields they established the first Baptist church on English ground and began propaganda in such ways as were open to them. Helwys soon found himself in Newgate prison, for he had brought with him from Holland a book he had written— *The Mistery of Iniquity*—which he began to circulate, and which insisted, for the first time in England, on the right of universal religious liberty. His bold and revolutionary words may fitly close this chapter. They indicate the point reached by these pioneers, after much perplexity and suffering. It was long before such convictions secured general acceptance, and only after much national tribulation. If they find a ready echo in democratic and liberty-loving nations to-day, it is because of the witness borne to them by a heroic succession of martyrs.

"Our Lord the King is but an earthly King, and he hath no aucthority as a King but in earthly causes, and if the King's people be obedient and true subjects, obeying all humane laws made by the King, our lord the King can require no more: for men's religion to God is betwixt God and themselves: the King shall not answere for it, neither may the King be jugd betwene God and Man. Let them be heretikes, Turcks, Jewes, or whatsoever, it apperteynes not to the earthly power to punish them in the least measure."[25]

[25] *The Mistery of Iniquity*, 1612, p. 69. On the subject of toleration see W. K. Jordan, *The Development of Religious Toleration in England*, Vol. I, to 1603 (1932); II, 1603-40 (1936); III and IV, 1640-60 (1938, 1940).

CHAPTER THREE

Struggle: The Seventeenth Century

The amazing importance of the struggle for religious
liberty is due partly to the momentous issue with which
it deals; but beyond that is the fact that it holds, as it
were in solution, within itself all the rest of the struggle
for liberty and equality.

A. S. P. WOODHOUSE,
Puritanism and Liberty, Intro., pp. 81-2.

THE LITTLE company of Separatists in the neighbourhood of Gainsborough, to which Smyth and Helwys
joined themselves, divided for the sake of convenience in
worshipping into two parts, the one in Gainsborough itself,
the other in the manor house at Scrooby. The latter had
considerable difficulty in getting to Holland. Among the
members were William Brewster, who lived at the manor
house, and John Robinson, a young clergyman, trained at
Cambridge in the fifteen-nineties, who, like so many others,
after much initial reluctance, had thrown in his lot with the
Separatists. After a few months in Amsterdam the Scrooby
group migrated, about a hundred strong, to Leyden, and
there formed a church on the Congregational pattern with
Robinson as pastor, and Brewster as ruling-elder. Robinson, though a vigorous controversialist, was a noble and
commanding figure, of wide outlook and lofty and benign
nature. The church in Leyden was singularly happy under
his leadership. News from England, however, was discon-
certing and made it clear that there was to be little chance

of religious freedom there while James I was on the throne. After the abortive Hampton Court Conference, some three hundred Puritan clergymen were driven from their livings. The thoughts of exiled Englishmen began to turn, as Penry had advised, towards America. Negotiations were opened with the king and the Virginia Company for permission to settle overseas. So it came about that early in 1620 a group of the younger members of the Leyden community, led by William Brewster, set out in the *Speedwell*. At Southampton they were joined by the *Mayflower* and a party of Puritans and Separatists from England. The *Speedwell* proved unseaworthy, and it was in the *Mayflower* that, on September 6th, the "Pilgrim Fathers", as they are now called, started on their hazardous and historic voyage across the Atlantic.

The importance of this enterprise for the subsequent history of America and the world in general cannot be exaggerated. It meant that Free Church principles were carried to the newly discovered continent and became the foundation of its life. Not all the Pilgrim Fathers were Separatists when they left England. The whole company covenanted together and combined "into a civil body politic" during the voyage, and avowed their continued loyalty to James I. Those from Leyden regarded themselves as still members of Robinson's church. But when at last the emigrants had established their settlements and reinforcements arrived from England and from Holland, a new church was formed, by covenant, and afterwards ministers and officers were chosen. The influence of Smyth and his Gainsborough covenant are clearly evident in what was done. In New England a fresh start was made with a self-governing religious community.

In taking leave of his friends when they left Leyden, Robinson used memorable words which still have a message.

They illustrate certain Free Church principles that deserve
constant emphasis, even though they have not always been
consistently adhered to, namely, belief in the guidance of the
Spirit, faith in private judgment, a sense of expectancy and
a willingness to experiment. These principles have had profound influence in many different spheres, particularly in the
New World. "I charge you," said Robinson, "that you
follow me no farther than you have seen me follow the Lord
Jesus Christ . . . I am verily persuaded, the Lord has more
Truth yet to break forth out of His holy Word. For my
part, I cannot sufficiently bewail the Condition of the
Reformed Churches, who are come to a Period in Religion
and will go at present no farther than the instruments of
their Reformation. The Lutheran can't be drawn to go
beyond what Luther saw . . . and the Calvinists, you see,
stick fast where they were left by that great Man of God,
who yet saw not all things. . . . I beseech you, remember,
'tis an Article of your Church Covenant, that *you be ready
to receive whatever Truth shall be made known to you from
the written Word of God*. . . . It is not possible the Christian World should come so lately out of such thick Anti-
christian Darkness, and that Perfection of Knowledge
should break forth at once."[1]

[1] Daniel Neal, *History of the Puritans*, Vol. II, 1732, p. 129. The
report is based on the 1646 account by Edward Winslow, one of those
who went out from Leyden. "This famous address," says Alexander
Gordon, *D.N.B.* XVII, p. 22, "recollected after twenty-six years or
more, owes something to the reporter's controversial needs." But it
rings true to Robinson's writings, and to the spirit of Smyth and
many others of the more radical pioneers. From a generation later
compare the striking passage written by John Goodwin, the Independent, in 1642, and quoted by Woodhouse, *op. cit.*, Intro., p. 46:
"If so great and considerable a part of the world as America is . . .
was yet unknown to all the world besides for so many generations
together, well may it be conceived . . . that . . . many truths, yea
and those of main concernment and importance, may be yet unborn
and not come forth out of their mother's womb—I mean the secrets

Within a few years in America, as in Holland and England, the claim was put forward for complete religious toleration, and infant baptism was rejected by many in favour of that of believers. Both developments found expression in a figure of outstanding importance, Roger Williams. Another son of Cambridge University, who, after a few years in the Established Church, had felt increasingly unhappy under its regimentation, Williams left England for America in 1630. In Massachusetts he soon found himself out of sympathy with the prevailing Puritan attempt at a Calvinist church-state, and, when threatened with arrest, escaped through the snows to Rhode Island where, in 1636, he planted a settlement on new lines, a settlement which was a landmark in human history with " as great liberties as any people under heaven ". " To Roger Williams," says Professor Bury, "belongs the glory of having founded the first modern State which was really tolerant and was based on the principle of taking the control of religious matters entirely out of the hands of the civil government."[2] Three years later Williams took the lead in founding the first Baptist church in America. One of his contemporaries said of him that he had " a windmill in his head ". Certainly he was excitable, outspoken and determined, but for his love of freedom, his concern for the

of the Scripture to see the light of the sun." On the importance of Goodwin, who was influenced by the Renaissance humanists, see Haller, *op. cit.*, pp. 199f., 370f. See also W. H. Burgess, *John Robinson*, 1920. On the story of the Pilgrim Fathers see G. F. Willison, *Saints and Strangers*, 1946.

[2] *History of Freedom of Thought*, p. 97. See A. B. Strickland, *Roger Williams: Prophet and Pioneer of Soul-Liberty*, 1919, and E. A. Payne, " Roger Williams: Apostle of Religious Freedom ", *Cong. Quarterly*, Vol. XIII, Oct., 1935. Nevins and Commager, *America, The Story of a Free People*, 1942, Ch. I. It has sometimes been claimed that the Torda Edict of Toleration, promulgated in 1568 by Prince Sigismund of Transylvania, antedates the action of Roger Williams.

Indians and his deep religious sincerity, he stands out as one of the most striking figures of his time. What he strove for in the Rhode Island Colony was to find its way ultimately into the American Constitution.

In the two decades between 1620 and 1640 some twenty thousand of the sturdiest folk in England made their way to the American colonies in the hope of finding there religious freedom. Most of them were of yeoman stock, with a sprinkling of artisans and indentured servants. Their ministers, and those who became magistrates, like the famous Governor Winthrop, were almost without exception university-trained men of good family. Laurence Binyon sang of them as

> " those adventurous ones who went
> Forth overseas, and, self-exiled,
> Sought from far isle and continent
> Another England in the wild,
> For whom no drums beat, yet they fought
> Alone, in courage of a thought
> Which an unbounded future wrought."[3]

Not all conceived freedom alike, but it was Puritan and Free Church principles in the widest sense that inspired them. The consequences we see in the general outlook of modern America with its " tenacious exaltation of liberty ".[4] There are echoes of Smyth and Robinson and Williams in the Declaration of Independence (1776) and in the twentieth-century speeches of Franklin D. Roosevelt.

[3] *England and Other Poems*, 1909.
[4] Nevins and Commager, *op. cit.*, 1942, p. vi. There was a further considerable emigration during the reign of Charles II, and this undoubtedly impoverished English Dissent in the subsequent decades. For American Puritanism in general see S. E. Morison, *Builders of the Bay Colony*, 1930, and the fine anthology by Perry Miller and T. H. Johnson, *The Puritans*, 1938.

II

The Pilgrim Fathers and their successors are worthy of the highest honour, but the debt of mankind is no less to those who stayed in England and there fought out the issue of religious, constitutional and civil liberty during the stormy days of the seventeenth century. Under Elizabeth the Puritans were a party in opposition to the Government policy, the Separatist pioneers but an apparently insignificant though troublesome minority. Few can have foreseen that, within forty years of the queen's death, there would be civil war, with the nation divided from end to end on the issues raised by the English Reformation settlement and the theory of the divine right of Kings by which the Stuarts sought to defend both their ecclesiastical and their political autocracy. Not a few writers, concentrating on the political aspect of affairs, and emphasizing the large measure of personal responsibility for what happened that must be borne by James I and Charles I, miss the deep religious motives that were at work throughout the land. " The England of the years in which Cromwell spent his active life," says Sir Ernest Barker, " the England of the years 1620 to 1660— was an England in a great mood of religious exaltation. This exaltation was not a show or a cloak or an hypocrisy; it was the genuine spirit of the age."[5]

During the early decades of the seventeenth century the Puritan party rapidly grew in strength and there was also a large increase in the number of Separatist churches. Many factors contributed to this. There was still much scandal and abuse among the clergy, the legacy of former times.

[5] *Oliver Cromwell*, p. 19. On the title page Sir Ernest Barker quotes the words of Acton : " It is no hyperbole to say that the progress of the world towards self-government would have been arrested but for the strength afforded by the religious motive in the seventeenth century."

Much of the strength of Puritanism came from the growing hatred of professional religion and the corruption it had brought in its train. "This," says Wakeman, "is the great mainstay of the Puritan and Nonconformist attack upon the Church, that she was the abettor and the propagator of abuses. It is the consciousness of moral superiority in that which appeared to them the most important of all moral duties, namely, unworldliness, that gave point to their denunciation."[6] Episcopacy seemed the buttress and defence of this unholy institution. So, with varying degrees of reluctance, it was felt by many that it must go. But the urgent moral compulsion that made men criticize the Church, and the ferment of new ideas which came from the Reformation, caused deep spiritual perplexity. This may be vividly illustrated by a sonnet written by Donne, who was Dean of St. Paul's from 1621 to 1631. Roman Catholics and Anglicans, Separatists and " Seekers " may all be identified in these lines.

> " Show me, dear Christ, Thy spouse, so bright and clear.
>   What! is it She, which on the other shore
>   Goes richly painted? or which rob'd and tore
>   Laments and mourns in Germany and here?
>   Sleeps she a thousand, then peeps up one year?
>   Is she self-truth and errs? now new, now outwore?
>   Doth she, and did she, and shall she evermore
>   On one, on seven, or on no hill appear?
>   Dwells she with us, or like adventuring Knights
>   First travel we to seek and then make Love?
>   Betray Kind Husband Thy spouse to our sights,
>   And let mine amorous soul court Thy mild Dove,
>   Who is most true and pleasing to Thee, then,
>   When she is embrac'd, and open to most men."[7]

[6] *History of the Church of England*, p. 57.
[7] I owe the reference to T. Lyon, *The Theory of Religious Liberty in England, 1603-39*, 1937.

The Puritans were many of them of the new middle class created by the social policy of the Tudors. In the struggle between Crown and Parliament they were allied with the business community. The Separatist pioneers, as we have seen, were most of them University men and well-connected. In the first half of the seventeenth century their ideas became a ferment in all ranks of society. These ideas, as they were further articulated and better understood, were seen to have considerable intrinsic appeal. There was instinctive reaction from the blundering and petulant obtuseness of James I, from the shifty scheming of his son, and from the savage penalties inflicted by Archbishop Laud in his zeal to enforce uniformity in worship and discipline. Professor Haller says that Laud's persecution of the Puritans was " badly managed, far from thorough, and in the long run, disas-trously ineffective ". The attack upon Puritan " lecture-ships " resulted in " the real beginning of independency as a positive influence in the unfolding of the revolutionary character of Puritanism ".[8] Further, there was an eager lay evangelism which stirred the common people in many parts of the country and particularly those who served in the " New Model " army. The ceaseless arguments and de-bates, the pamphlet warfare, as well as the grimmer episodes of imprisonment, torture, and finally, open conflict, led to many extravagances; but out of all the confusion the general shape of things to come gradually emerged. A considerable section of the community decided in favour of a Free Church approach to the problems both of Church and State.

The development of public opinion may be seen by study-ing the records of the Westminster Assembly, which gathered in 1643 to carry through " a due and necessary reformation of the Government and Liturgy of the Church ", or those of the Army debates of 1647-9, or those

[8] *Op. cit.*, p. 231.

of the associations and assemblies of Baptists and Independents which met in the closing years of the Protectorate. The influential Westminster Assembly came together at the time when Parliament had finally lost patience with Charles I and when Strafford and Laud had been impeached for treason. It pledged itself to Presbyterianism of the Genevan and Scottish kind, and drew up a thoroughly Calvinistic Confession of Faith. But it was still anxious for uniformity and endeavoured to suppress all other forms of worship and belief, sectarian as well as Anglican. Its temper is not unfairly set out in a communication sent by the Scottish General Assembly to the English Parliament in 1642: "We now look for a perfect and thorough reformation: all may resort to the same public worship, and the name of Heresies and Sectaries, Puritans, Conformists, Separatists and Anabaptists may be suppressed. The prelatical hierarchy being put out of the way, the work will be easy." There were, however, five "Dissenting brethren" at the Assembly, who received the name "Independents", since, in opposition to the presbyterian system they maintained the right of every congregation to govern itself. They defended their views on the basis of scripture, and though the majority rejected their case, often with some heat, yet the Assembly gave them a most valuable platform. It was soon clear that they represented a very considerable body of opinion in the country.

The Army debates of a few years later show the strength not only of the Presbyterians and the Independents, but also of those who have been called "the Parties of the left", the more radical both in politics and religion.[9] It was these

[9] See A. S. P. Woodhouse, *Puritanism and Liberty. Debates from the Clarke MSS. with Supplementary Documents*, 1938, and for the whole paragraph compare G. P. Gooch, *English Democratic Ideas in the Seventeenth Century*, 1898 (second edition, with supplementary notes and appendices by H. J. Laski, 1927), T. C. Pease, *The Leveller*

more revolutionary groups—even Levellers, Fifth Monarchy Men and Diggers—who most effectively held aloft the banner of religious freedom, and with it that of civil liberty and equality. The Levellers were advanced democrats, whose aims were as much secular as religious. The Fifth Monarchy movement seems to have originated among the Baptists: it aimed at the establishment of the reign of Christ and His saints, appealing to Daniel ii. 44. The Diggers, led by Everard and Winstanley, were a genuine proletarian movement of the dispossessed with communist tendencies. All these movements indicate the ferment of ideas that were at work and which helped to produce men like George Fox and John Bunyan. The main groups of Nonconformists were of a more sober type. They also had rapidly increased. At the Savoy, in 1658, two hundred delegates met from one hundred and twenty Independent or Congregational churches to frame a Declaration of Faith and Order, and to show that they were not " like so many ships . . . launched singly, and sailing apart and alone in the vast ocean of these tumultuous times . . . but a fleet making together for the same port ". There were considerable numbers of Baptists in Cromwell's army, and groups of Baptist churches in different parts of the country associated together for common purposes.

It is impossible here to follow in detail the religious and political conflicts of the Civil War and Commonwealth

Movement, 1916, D. M. Wolfe, *Leveller Manifestoes of the Puritan Revolution*, 1944, W. Haller and G. Davies, *The Leveller Tracts*, 1945, L. F. Brown, *The Political Activities of Baptists and Fifth Monarchy Men*, 1912, G. H. Sabine, *The Works of Gerrard Winstanley*, 1941, L. Hamilton, *Selections from the Works of Winstanley*, 1945, M. A. Gibb, *John Lilburne the Leveller*, 1947, and W. Schenk, *Social Justice in the Puritan Revolution*, 1948. The last named represents a welcome reaction from the attempt of Marxist writers like E. Bernstein and D. W. Petergorsky to discount the religious element in radical Puritanism.

periods. A few points only can be made, in the most summary fashion. The attempt to establish the Presbyterian kind of Puritanism failed. The nation adjudged, with Milton, that " new presbyter is but old priest writ large ". The voice of England spoke in judgment upon the Stuarts in the person of Oliver Cromwell, and he was the incarnation of Independency, a deeply religious man for whom religious freedom was more important than political freedom. On any showing he is one of the greatest figures in English history. Though the system he established failed to survive him, yet his pleas for toleration, which were in advance of his time and even of his party, and his passionate desire for national righteousness, entered into the English heritage. Cromwell had to depend much on the sword, yet he appealed to the plain man, respected him and trusted his judgment. " The consciences of common men were a new phenomenon in politics," says Professor Woodhouse, " and one that has never disappeared."[10]   Side by side with this may be set the observation of Firth, that, thanks to Cromwell, " Nonconformity had time to take root and to grow so strong in England that the storm which followed the Restoration had no power to root it up."[11] Nor must we forget the ever memorable plea of Milton, the great Puritan poet, Latin secretary of the Council of State from 1649 to 1660 : " Give me the liberty to know, to utter, and to argue freely according to conscience, above all liberties."[12]

III

Had Cromwell lived a few years longer the subsequent

[10] *Op. cit.*, p. 53.
[11] Quoted by Barker, *Oliver Cromwell*, p. 46. Cf. G. M. Trevelyan, *An Autobiography*, 1949, p. 167 : " The heart of English Puritanism down the ages has proved to be sectarian and individualist, not Presbyterian : there Cromwell was right and his work outlived him."
[12] *Areopagitica*, 1644.

history of England might have been a very different one. But he died in 1658, leaving only a weak son to succeed him. To avoid anarchy, Parliament recalled Charles II (son of Charles I) from his exile. There was some hope that he might have profited by the example of his father and might understand the deep desire of Englishmen for order and freedom, both religious and political. But he was a Stuart. There was an inevitable royalist reaction, and though there was no general revenge upon the Roundhead Party, yet scapegoats were found in the Puritan Nonconformists, and Clarendon, Charles's minister, gave his name to a savage penal code against them.

The Act of Uniformity of 1662 is by many taken as the real beginning of Nonconformity. It insisted on the necessity of episcopal ordination; it restored the Anglican Prayer Book and ejected from their livings any clergy who would not give their "unfeigned consent and assent" to everything the book contained. Some two thousand suffered in this way, many of them enduring much personal hardship.[13] The great majority were Presbyterians, who, during the Commonwealth, had secured parishes, and who represented the older Puritan tradition of reform. They went bravely out into the wilderness, though many of them would not have been averse to a church establishment of their own devising, and not a few believed in only a limited religious toleration. Some two hundred, perhaps fewer, were Congregationalists or Independents, who, under Cromwell, had secured parish livings. Those thus ejected swelled the number of Separatists, Baptists and others, already outside the Established Church and still liable to suffer under unrepealed Elizabethan legislation.[14]

[13] A. G. Matthews, *Calamy Revised*, 1934, gives notes of the careers of 1,760 of the ejected, but his study does not cover the four Welsh dioceses.

[14] Cf. H. W. Clark, *op. cit.*, II, p. 35 : " Perhaps for the historian

We cannot date Nonconformity from 1662 without over-
looking the courageous witness of the more radical groups
during the previous decades, though it has sometimes been
claimed that these would have been relatively easy to suppress had they not been joined by the victims of the Act of
Uniformity and the further Acts which followed. Professor
Trevelyan has weighty words in this connection: " The
religious settlement of the Restoration was not conceived in
the spirit of compromise which marked the political and
social settlement. Yet it may at least be questioned whether
it has not led to more religious, intellectual and political
liberty than would have resulted from a wider extension of
the boundaries of the Established Church. If the plan to
' comprehend ' Baxter and the moderate Puritans had succeeded at the abortive Savoy Conference of 1661, the
Quakers, Baptists, and more advanced sects, which must
still have been left outside, might have been too isolated and
inconsiderable ever to enforce the claim of toleration for
themselves."[15]

Of the Clarendon Code the most important acts were a
new Conventicle Act, making illegal meetings for worship
where the family was joined by more than five persons, and
the Five Mile Act, which drove the ejected ministers from
the towns where they had preached, and prevented their
having schools—with most unfortunate and far-reaching
effects on Puritan culture. It is no excuse for this legislation
—reminiscent as it is of more modern anti-religious codes—
to say that it was prompted by fear of insurrection against

of the fortunes of the true Nonconformist ideal, the most important
thing about the Act of Uniformity of 1662 is the fact that it linked
together a Presbyterianism only superficially and by accident Nonconformist and an Independency which, though essentially and truly
Nonconformist, had already fallen in no small measure from its
earliest high estate."

[15] *History of England*, p. 450. Cf. C. E. Whiting, *Studies in
English Puritanism*, 1931.

the throne. The charge of treason and the cry that the State is in danger have too often been used against those whose desire is simply to worship in freedom. The Clarendon Code, like many other similar enactments before and since, proved unsuccessful in its aim. " Now began the romance of Nonconformity," says Adeney, " fascinating to read about, but tragic to experience. Meetings were held in lonely houses, in cellars, in hay-lofts, in all sorts of out-of-the-way places. Secret passages were provided and watchers were set to give notice of the danger of arrest."[16]

War with Holland caused Charles II—who was at heart a Roman Catholic—to issue in 1672 an indulgence to " tender consciences ", to win him support from both Roman Catholics and Nonconformists. But Parliament objected to this largely personal act of clemency and passed the Test Act of 1673, which insisted that every official of the crown from the highest to the lowest should renounce the doctrine of transubstantiation and receive the Lord's Supper at his parish church. This excluded from the public service all Nonconformists and Roman Catholics. It remained on the statute book till 1828 and contributed greatly to the formality which characterized much eighteenth-century religion. From 1673 till Charles II died in 1685, and throughout the troubled reign of James II, much depended on local conditions how vigorously Free Churchmen were persecuted. In some places their sufferings were most severe, and in Dorset and Somerset, in 1685-6, after the ineffectual attempt of the Duke of Monmouth to get the throne from James II, many new pages were written in the records of Nonconformist martyrdoms thanks to the ruthless cruelty of Judge Jeffreys. " In the general horror felt at the long rows of tarred and gibbeted Dissenters along the roadsides of Wessex," says

[16] *Encyclopedia of Religion and Ethics*, IX, p. 389.

Trevelyan, " came the first recoil from the mutual rage of parties that had so long devastated English political and religious life, the first instinctive movement towards a new era of national unity and toleration."[17]

For two or three more years James II pursued his tortuous and tyrannical path, but he gradually antagonized even the Tory Party and the Anglican Church. Moreover, the revocation of the Edict of Nantes by the Roman Catholic, Louis XIV of France, and the hideous cruelty with which he attacked the Huguenots,[18] brought to England, as to Holland and Prussia, tens of thousands of refugees, many of them artisans and merchants of ability and character. They formed a most stimulating element in English life, strengthened the hatred of " Popery " in this country and contributed a new influence to the Protestant and Free Church tradition. James continued to bid one party off against another, and ignored more and more flagrantly the constitutional limits of his authority. At last leaders from all sections of English political life joined to invite the Protestant prince, William of Orange (a grandson of Charles I, and married to James II's daughter, Mary) to come and take the throne.

The " Glorious Revolution " of 1688-9 owed its glory to its bloodlessness, to the relief with which it was received. It had the support of the vast majority of the community who were as sick of the involved and bitter religious and political controversies of the preceding decades as they were

[17] *History of England*, p. 467. G. Lyon Turner, *Original Records of Early Nonconformity*, 1911, gives full details of the licences obtained under the various indulgences.

[18] The name was originally spelt " Hugonots " and seems to have come from Tours, where the favourite meeting-place of these French evangelicals, who traced their origin back to Calvin, was the gate of St. Hugon. See *Encyclopedia of Religion and Ethics*, VI, article " Huguenots " by W. T. Whitley, and A. J. Grant, *The Huguenots*, 1934.

of the Stuarts. It laid down the main lines along which English life was to run for the next century and a half. The Toleration Act passed in 1689 was anomalous, but at least it brought to an end the active persecution of Dissenters and accepted them as an element likely to be permanent and entitled to some recognition. It may be said to have involved toleration but not full liberty of conscience, much less real religious equality. It did not allow dissent from the accepted doctrinal standards of the Church. Nor did Dissenters at first desire this, though a few among them already objected to the principle of subscription. All Nonconformist preachers and teachers were required to subscribe to the Anglican Articles of Religion with the exception of numbers 34, 35 and 36, that is, those dealing with the tradition of the Church, the public reading of the second Book of Homilies and episcopal ordination. An attempt was made, before the Act was passed, to undo the effects of 1662 so far as Presbyterians were concerned, but, though led by Baxter, it proved unsuccessful. The Anglican Church continued as the Established Church, and religious tests remained for public offices. Nevertheless Nonconformists were granted the right to worship in their own way, though they had to register their meeting-houses and were subject to a number of other restrictions.

The success of the witness borne by the Separatists and their successors during the previous century was seen in the readiness there now was to admit the necessity of religious toleration, and also in the large number of Nonconformist groups which immediately secured licences[19] and proceeded to erect meeting-houses. Nonconformity could no longer be equated with civil disobedience. From the very beginning, as Trevelyan puts it, " the spirit of the Toleration

[19] Shillito, p. 31, gives the number of registrations from 1688-1700 as 2,418.

Act was practised much more widely than the letter war-
ranted ".[20] Within the twenty years that followed 1689,
nearly one thousand chapels were built. The majority of
them were for Presbyterians, then came those for Baptists,
with the Independents a good third.[21]

By the end of the seventeenth century the various factors
which we have briefly noticed had come together to shape
the main Free Church bodies. The Puritans, the Separatists,
the radicals of the Commonwealth period, the Presbyterians
and Independents driven from the Established Church in
1662, all had their part in creating a considerable body of
informed and convinced religious opinion which believed in
simplicity and freedom in worship, which rejected episcopal
government, and which declined the advantages of State
support.

IV

The rich contribution made to the English tradition by
the early generations of Free Churchmen will already have
become clear. We may see it vividly illustrated by recalling
four outstanding seventeenth-century figures who are still
gratefully remembered and continue to exercise a considerable influence on the thinking and practice of large sections
of the Christian Church—Richard Baxter, John Owen,
George Fox and John Bunyan.[22] All save Bunyan were

[20] *Op. cit.*, p. 474. Cf. A. Gordon, *Freedom after Ejection: 1690-
92*, 1917.
[21] F. J. Powicke, *Essays Congregational and Catholic*, 1931, p. 301.
[22] Writings of Baxter, Fox and Bunyan will be found in the Everyman Library. There is no modern study of Owen, but note *The
Golden Book of John Owen* (edited by J. Moffatt, 1904). For the
others see F. J. Powicke, *A Life of the Rev. Richard Baxter*, 1924,
and *Richard Baxter under the Cross*, 1927; W. C. Braithwaite, *The
Beginnings of Quakerism*, 1912, and *The Second Period of Quakerism*, 1919; A. N. Brayshaw, *The Personality of George Fox*, 1933;
John Brown, *John Bunyan*, 1885, Tercentenary Edition, 1928.

born in the reign of James I, and he only a few years later. Owen lived on to experience more than twenty years of the Stuart Restoration; Bunyan died in James II's reign; Baxter and Fox survived to see, as old men, the religious settlement of William III. All four left extensive literary remains. Baxter, Fox and Bunyan told their own stories in works that have become religious classics.

Though he had not the spiritual stature of the other three, we may begin with Owen because his influence was the earliest and he played his part in the centre of the political and religious arena. An Oxford man by training, he had to leave the University owing to Laud's severe measures against those with Puritan sympathies, but secured an Essex living at the outbreak of the Civil War and soon passed, under the influence of a pamphlet that came from America, to Congregationalist views. He became Cromwell's chaplain and trusted friend for many years, and was with him in Ireland. From 1651-60 he was Dean of Christ Church, Oxford, and for most of that time Vice-Chancellor, doing much to restore the dignity and glory of the University. His learning and prestige made him the natural leader of the Savoy Conference of Independents and Congregationalists in 1658. Early in 1660 he was removed from Christ Church in favour of a Presbyterian. Unlike many of those who were ejected in 1662, he had considerable private means. He lived for a time in Oxford and was indicted under the Conventicle Act in 1665 for holding religious assemblies. Soon after, he moved to London and busied himself with writing in defence of Nonconformist principles. Charles II's Declaration of Indulgence enabled him to preach again, and he apparently secured some measure of royal confidence and favour, being entrusted by the King with one thousand guineas for his poorer ministerial brethren. When he died in 1683, the carriages of some sixty noblemen and a vast concourse of people attended the funeral in Bunhill Fields. Dr. F. J. Powicke thinks that, after 1662, Owen led Independency astray.[23] He should have promoted rapprochement with the Presbyterians, who, under Baxter's influence, were ready for compromise. Instead, he maintained and even hardened his views against bishops and against liturgical worship. His was indeed a somewhat rigid Calvinism. He placed considerable emphasis on orthodoxy, and was vigorous in controversy with Socinians and Quakers as well as with Roman Catholics. Powicke ascribes his failure in large part to his " reverence for the letter of Scripture ". Bibliolatry is certainly a sin, but Baxter and his friends still looked for comprehension within a national church. Owen stood for " the gathered Church ", and his work *The True Nature of a Gospel Church and its Government* contains an exposition of this standpoint which still exerts considerable influence.

Richard Baxter was described by S. R. Gardiner as " the most learned and moderate of the Dissenters ". He stands out amid the turbulent currents of his time, an ascetic figure of uncompromising honesty and courage, a cross-bench mind of considerable philosophic power, a preacher and pastor who steadily advanced in authority and influence, but who left behind him not so much great practical achievements as the memory of saintliness and personal devotion. He came of a well-connected family and was for a short time at Court. After ordination he taught and " lectured " in Shropshire and Worcestershire. When the Civil War broke out, after some hesitation he joined the Parliamentary side and served as a chaplain in the West Country. Returning to Kidderminster in 1647, whilst battling against almost constant ill-health, he preached—in his own phrase, which had much more than his physical condition in mind—" as a dying man

[23] *Essays, Congregational and Catholic*, pp. 297-301.

to dying men ", wrote his *Reformed Pastor* and *The Saints' Everlasting Rest*, which have continued to speak to the hearts and consciences of men,[24] encouraged the evangelistic work of John Eliot among the Red Indians and sought to meet the spiritual needs of his time with a deep concern for the purity of the Church and a deep respect for her ancient traditions. When the Restoration took place, his personal prestige was such that Charles II appointed him chaplain-in-ordinary and offered him a bishopric, if he would conform. Baxter used all his influence to find some way of " comprehension " which would lead back Presbyterians and Independents into the National Church. Though he was the recognized spokesman of the former party, he was himself in reality a moderate Episcopalian, fearing schism and desiring the widest Christian fellowship. " Look on all particular churches as members of the universal," he said in 1659, " and choose the best thou canst for thy *ordinary communion*. . . . But deny not *occasional communion* with any (though accused by others) further than they force thee to sin or than they separate from Christ." Such views were too broad and tolerant for Baxter's generation and his comprehension proposals failed. The Act of Uniformity drove him from the Church of England, and he suffered considerable personal ill-treatment during the latter part of Charles II's reign. Within a few months of James II's accession the infamous Judge Jeffreys issued a warrant for the arrest of Baxter on the charge of covertly attacking the civil and religious

[24] e.g. Hensley Henson, *Retrospect of an Unimportant Life*, I, 1943, p. 38: " It is literally true that Baxter's *Pastor* and *Autobiography* gave colour and direction to my efforts." A modern abridgment of *The Reformed Pastor*, with a valuable introductory essay, was edited by J. T. Wilkinson in 1939. For Baxter's ethics, see Tawney, *Religion and the Rise of Capitalism*, 1926, and R. B. Schlatter, *The Social Ideas of Religious Leaders, 1660-88*, 1940. See also I. Morgan, *The Nonconformity of Richard Baxter*, 1946.

authorities in a paraphrase of the New Testament. " We
have had to do with other sorts of persons," cried Jeffreys
when Baxter was before him, " but now we have a saint to
deal with: and I know how to deal with saints as well as
sinners." He is said to have urged that the seventy-year-old
man should be whipped through the city, but in the end
Baxter escaped with seventeen months in prison, and lived
on in London to welcome William III, and to accept such
benefits as the Toleration Act of 1689 gave to Nonconformists, though still dreaming of a wider and more comprehensive Church.

Owen and Baxter came of the ruling class. With Fox and
Bunyan we have products of the great religious ferment
which went on among the humble folk of the English
country-side. Fox was a Leicestershire weaver, Bunyan a
Bedfordshire tinker. If any real justification of Nonconformist principles were still needed, it might be sought in
the careers of these two men. They demonstrated by their
religious power and insight that the grace of God and the
true spirit of prophecy are not tied to the traditional channels
of church or sacrament. Of Fox, Trevelyan says that he
" made at least the most original contribution to the history
of religion of any Englishman ";[25] while it has been well
said of Bunyan: " There can be no hesitation in placing him
among the great modifying forces of our culture. It would
be hard to find a single figure, at least in our religious
history, who has contributed so much to the immensely
complicated process which has made us what we are."[26]
Both of these men came from the more radical wing of
the Puritan movement. During their early spiritual
struggles both were in touch with Baptist communities.
Bunyan indeed is often claimed as a Baptist, though his

[25] *Op. cit.*, p. 431.
[26] L. P. Jacks, *The Times*, November 22nd, 1928.

views of church fellowship led him to regard " differences of judgment about water baptism " as " no bar to communion ".[27] He began thereby a tradition in the south Midlands of churches in which Baptists and Paedo-Baptists were members together. Fox was the founder of a unique religious movement.

During the Civil War, Fox, then a young man in his early twenties, wandered about the Midlands unsuccessfully seeking spiritual guidance and peace from various Puritan teachers. He came at length to believe in direct personal inspiration, in the Inner Light. Christ, he believed, spoke to him " without the help of any man, book or writing ". He was soon at work preaching and gathering into little companies " Friends of Truth ", who within a few months received the nickname Quakers because of the physical excitement which often accompanied their experiences. Fox was soon in collision with the ecclesiastical authorities and found himself in prison first in one place and then in another. His dramatic entry into Lichfield on a winter's day without shoes, and crying, " Woe unto the bloody city of Lichfield," illustrates his strange spiritual exaltation. He travelled widely throughout England and Scotland, and later in Ireland, America and on the Continent. A number of times he had meetings with Cromwell during the last four years of the latter's life, and clearly much impressed him. But the Quakers suffered badly at the hands of the Presbyterians, and more severely still after the Restoration. Between 1660 and 1689 more than 12,000 were imprisoned, thirty-two of whom died while in custody. Moreover, there was vigorous controversy both in America and England with Congregationalists and Baptists, though it was among the Puritan sectaries generally that, in the second half of the century, Quakers won striking success. Their discarding of

[27] See Bunyan's treatise with this title, 1673.

E

Church organization and outward sacrament, as well as their pacifist leanings, were little understood or appreciated by most of their contemporaries. Fox, however, won to his views a number of distinguished converts, the most notable being Robert Barclay, a gifted young Scot with royal connections, and William Penn, son of Admiral Sir William Penn.[28] While at Oxford young Penn had been influenced by John Owen in his last months as Dean of Christ Church. No one did more than Penn to raise the name and establish the ideals of the Society of Friends on both sides of the Atlantic, and to set the lines along which they were to serve future generations of the Christian Church.

While Fox was seeking enlightenment and Owen and Baxter were serving as military chaplains, young John Bunyan was a private soldier among the forces of the Parliamentary Army. The war over, he returned to his tinkering and went through years of spiritual struggle and distress even more intense than fell to the lot of Fox. They are graphically and movingly described in *Grace Abounding to the Chief of Sinners*, one of the greatest of religious autobiographies. Bunyan found Luther's Commentary on Galatians " (excepting the Holy Bible) beyond all books that ever I have seen . . . most fit for wounded consciences ". He went through a rich evangelical experience and in 1653 joined himself to a group of Bedford Nonconformists. Before long he was preaching in the neighbourhood to the chagrin of the order-loving Presbyterian clergymen of the Commonwealth. His first imprisonment took place under the unrepealed Elizabethan Act of Uniformity. Clarendon's legislation kept him in prison for nearly twelve years,

[28] See Bonamy Dobrée, *William Penn, Quaker and Pioneer*, 1932, and the Everyman volume of Penn's writings. He wrote *No Cross No Crown* in 1668 while imprisoned in the Tower, being then twenty-five years old. E. E. Taylor, *The Valiant Sixty*, 1947, gives an attractive picture of the first Quaker preachers.

but during that time he began writing, in simple, vigorous language which draws its effectiveness and purity from his study of the English Bible. Charles II's Declaration of Indulgence benefited Bunyan temporarily, as it did Owen and Baxter, but in 1675 he was back in prison, and there wrote the immortal *Pilgrim's Progress*, which is now accepted as a religious classic by all branches of the Christian Church, its allegorical figures and its imagery familiar and dear to Anglicans as well as Nonconformists, to Americans as well as Englishmen. In the last years of his life Bunyan had freedom to preach. Then, as ever, he could claim, "I preached what I felt, what I smartingly did feel," and throughout the southern Midlands and the Home Counties and in London he was widely known. More than a thousand people would congregate before seven o'clock on a winter's morning to hear him, and it was while on a preaching visit to London in 1688 that he died.

All these men were great Englishmen—loyal Englishmen. Frequent charges of treason were made against them, charges which now sound somewhat fantastic. Yet it was their faithfulness to their own consciences which broadened the whole conception of freedom in this country. They strove valiantly as they did because of their deep religious convictions, for though they were great Englishmen and great Nonconformists they are now universally regarded as even greater Christians, and in a true apostolic succession. Take away Milton and Cromwell, Owen and Baxter, Fox and Bunyan from the records of seventeenth-century England and what living voices remain? Jeremy Taylor and Sir Thomas Browne? The Cambridge Platonists? These are fainter voices, whereas the others still speak directly to our modern need in language that the simplest may understand.

CHAPTER FOUR

Recognition: 1689-1750

Both the Church of England and the Dissenter suffer
in their Reputation for the mixt Multitude of their
Members which is occasioned by the present Prosperity.
. . . Methinks Men should seem what they are: if a
man Dissent from the Church, let him do so; and his
Principle being well-grounded for such Dissent, let him
hold it: if not well-grounded, let him leave it: if he
cannot suffer one way, let him suffer another; and why
should we not be as honest to God as our country.

DANIEL DEFOE,
A Discourse upon Occasional Conformity,
1701, pp. 12 and 23.

SINCE THE time of Goldsmith the period centring in
the reign of Queen Anne (1702-14) has been known as the
English " Augustan Age ". It was certainly a time of rare
literary brilliance. Dryden died in 1700, and already Swift
and Addison were writing. These two were soon joined by
Steele, Pope, Gay, and Prior. Defoe was busy with his
pamphlets, and in 1719 *Robinson Crusoe* was to appear.
Berkeley wrote the more important of his philosophical
works during the opening decade of the eighteenth century,
and in 1713 he came from Ireland and associated with the
English *littérateurs*. Isaac Watts began the publication of
his hymns in the same period, though it can hardly be
described as a time of deep religious feeling. On the contrary, the temper of the age favoured moderation in all
things. Good form seemed more attractive than enthusiasm.

68

Outward manners and respectability hid a decline in morals. There was widespread reaction from the religious controversies of the preceding century. The Toleration Act of 1689 had confirmed the Anglican Church in power but had given some limited recognition to Dissenters. Both parties, therefore, enjoyed a measure of prosperity; both parties failed to withstand the searching tests that prosperity brings.

In the years that are our special concern in this chapter, three matters occupied much of the attention and energy of the religious bodies: first, their mutual relations, secondly, the particular problem of what was called " occasional conformity ", and, thirdly, theological issues connected with subscription to the Thirty-nine Articles and the Westminster Catechism.

Reference has already been made to attempts both in 1661 and 1690 to broaden the basis of the Established Church so as to regain at any rate Presbyterians and Independents. These attempts failed, partly because of the limited vision of those in authority, but more because of the intransigence of the Anglicans regarding episcopacy and the unreadiness of Nonconformists to surrender their hardly won freedom. Both sides had their bigots and fanatics. The High Churchmen liked to think of Dissenters as " still Commonwealth men, king-killers, dangerous and gloomy fanatics who were only prevented from helping chaos to come again by the weakness of their numbers and the strong laws which kept them in check ".[1] With Anne on the throne, Churchmen seemed to have a fine opportunity of strengthening their own position and undoing the results of William III's generally friendly attitude towards their opponents. There was a

[1] James Sutherland, *Defoe*, 1937, p. 80. See Lincoln, *English Dissent, 1763-1800*, 1938, p. 5, for evidence of similar charges in the second half of the century.

considerable drift from Nonconformity back to the Church on the part of those desiring public office and unable to face the social and educational penalties of Dissent. Then, as at other times, the children of staunch Nonconformists failed to appreciate their parents' convictions and preferred to take the less strenuous way of the majority. Nor were these the only motives. There was often a genuine desire to render public and patriotic service and almost every avenue was closed to avowed Dissenters.

This conforming movement, however, was not nearly as rapid or widespread as many Churchmen had hoped and anticipated. Moreover, there had grown up during the closing years of William III the practice of " occasional conformity " by which, by attending the communion service at the parish church just previous to election to office, a Nonconformist was held to fulfil the letter of the law. It is right to note that by no means all Nonconformists were ready for such compromising, and that the Baptists in particular stood out against it.[2] Nevertheless, the practice became sufficiently general for Churchmen and Tories to endeavour to end it. Again and again during Anne's reign an Occasional Conformity Bill was presented, the terms of which were so stringent that they clearly aimed at preventing Nonconformists having any part in the national life and so at achieving their gradual extinction. The Bill was long opposed by the Whigs who accepted in general the position advocated by John Locke: Let there be an established church, but with

[2] See H. W. Clark, *op. cit.*, II, p. 146. Milner, *Life of Watts*, p. 319, makes clear the patriotic motives that inspired men like Sir Thomas Abney, Lord Mayor of London. But Abney was driven for a time to cease attending his usual place of worship and to rely on a domestic chaplain who was a Nonconformist minister. In those who maintained the Baxter tradition there was a religious motive for occasional conformity. Cf. p. 63 above and p. 116 below; Henry Rogers, *Life of John Howe*, 1862, pp. 297ff.; and Shute Barrington, *Principles of an Occasional Conformist*, 1718.

the widest practicable comprehension and the general tolerance of all save atheists and Roman Catholics. Locke had
been at Christ Church under John Owen, and though he
reacted from the Puritanism of his youth, yet he agreed with
Hobbes that most of the ills of the seventeenth century were
due to a priesthood that was corrupt and that had power
outside its proper sphere. In 1711 political considerations
led the Whigs to abate their opposition and an Occasional
Conformity Act was passed. It was followed in 1714 by a
Schism Act, aimed at the schools and academies of the Dissenters, which, had it been enforced, would have prevented
any effective education by Nonconformists. But the very
day the Act was to become law Queen Anne died. It is
hardly surprising that many harassed Nonconformists interpreted their deliverance as a direct intervention of the
Almighty. In the changes that came with the accession of
George I their position was secured and no further attempts
to go back upon the Toleration Act of 1689 have been
seriously made, though more than a century had to pass
before the legal rights of Nonconformists were extended.

The general attitude of Dissenters in the decade thus
briefly surveyed may be judged by reading Swift's biting
satire, *The Tale of a Tub*, which, though written about 1697,
did not appear till 1704. In it he tells the story of three
brothers who each received from their father a coat with
strict injunctions against any alteration; Peter stands for the
Roman Church, Martin for the Anglican, and Jack for the
dissenting descendants of John Calvin. It is against Peter
that the satire is most vigorous. Jack is treated with coarse
contempt. How easily public opinion might be stirred
against Nonconformists may be seen also in the popular
excitement which followed the scurrilous sermons of Dr.
Henry Sacheverell and in the occasional outbreaks of mob
violence against dissenting meeting-houses, of which there

are records from several parts of the country. Nonconformists had few advocates in high places, though Defoe,
writing in his famous *Review* in 1712, estimated that they
numbered in all two millions.[3]

Defoe himself is an interesting figure, a typical product of
the age in many respects. His father, who was a tallow-
chandler, was a member of Dr. Samuel Annesley's congregation at St. Giles, Cripplegate. Annesley represented the
older type of Presbyterian divine. He had been no friend
of Cromwell's, yet in 1662 he was among the ejected. After
Charles II's Declaration of Indulgence, he began preaching
at a meeting-house in Bishopsgate. Defoe was therefore
brought up a Dissenter. He was educated at a Dissenting
Academy. He married the daughter of a well-to-do Dissenting merchant. He seems, indeed, to have been deeply
influenced by Annesley, whose chief claim to remembrance
to-day lies in the fact that one of his twenty-four children
was Susanna, mother of John and Charles Wesley. Defoe's
Puritanism, it has been said, " is a very real part of his
strange character: but, compared with that of a man like
John Bunyan, it is of an inferior type, and it burns at times
with a very greasy flame ".[4] Nevertheless, occasional con-
conformity offended him—" playing Bo-peep with God
Almighty ", he scathingly called it—and when Sacheverell
and others advocated further repressive measures, Defoe
wrote *The Shortest Way with Dissenters*, in which he tried
the dangerous game of ridiculing his opponents by urging
the total suppression of Dissent at any cost. The pamphlet
led to his being fined, imprisoned and set in the pillory, but

[3] The membership of their churches at this time is usually estimated at about 200,000 and Defoe's figure must have included all
those whom he thought sympathetic to the Dissenters. Cf. Halévy,
III, 50-1; Lincoln, *English Dissent*, p. 15; Bebb, *Nonconformity and
Social and Economic Life*, 1935, Ch. II.
[4] Sutherland, *op. cit.*, p. 211.

on this occasion he had popular feeling with him.[5] There
is a tradition that Defoe himself sometimes preached. His
methods and the strange vicissitudes of his life did not com-
mend him to the graver sort of Nonconformist. But he
never repudiated the name, even if looked on with suspicion
by those whose cause he championed, and even if a stranger
to the deeper things of religion.

Among themselves Nonconformists were by no means all
in agreement either about public affairs or denominational
matters. Presbyterian and Independent ministers—the
larger groups among the " ejected "—drew up in 1690 certain
" Heads of Agreement ", which aimed at a union. It was
a kind of compromise or amalgam of their different polities,
but it was wrecked almost at once by doctrinal controversies
in which it became clear that, theologically, the Independents remained the more orthodox Calvinists, and that the
Presbyterians were the more infected with the spirit of free
inquiry and with rationalist tendencies. The stage was
already being prepared for the Deist movement of the
eighteenth century and for the arguments about the Trinity
which occupied so much of the attention of the theologians
in all the churches. The Baptists were engaged not only in
controversies regarding doctrine—having an Arminian as
well as a Calvinist wing—but also in disputes about congregational hymn-singing, in which certain of their number
were pioneers. Presbyterians, Independents and Baptists
began to draw somewhat closer together than they had been
before, though their differences were still very apparent.
The Quakers, like the other bodies, had lost the spiritual
exaltation of the previous century. They carried on a costly
fight against the paying of tithes, but were divided among
themselves as to organization and discipline.

[5] The pamphlet is included in A. C. Ward, *A Miscellany of Tracts
and Pamphlets*, World's Classics, 1927.

II

The death of Queen Anne is said to have been first publicly announced in an Independent Chapel in Fetter Lane. During the sermon a messenger from Bishop Burnet leant over the gallery and dropped a handkerchief—which had been the prearranged signal. The preacher said nothing of the event, which meant so much to Nonconformists, but in his closing prayer prayed for " George, King of Great Britain and Ireland ". The congregation, deeply moved, joined in the eighty-ninth Psalm which begins:

" I will sing of the mercies of the Lord for ever:
    With my mouth will I make known Thy faithfulness
        to all generations."[6]

It was a great deliverance that had come to them and they were sensible of it.

The House of Hanover secured the throne of England, but for some time their tenure of it was by no means certain. In Oxford, Birmingham, Norwich and elsewhere, there were popular riots at the time of the accession and corona- tion of George I, and the mob expressed their feelings at the expense of the Nonconformists. In 1715 the Old Pretender made a brief bid for popular support assisted by Scots who hoped to re-establish Scottish independence, and by Roman Catholics of the North of England. Nonconformists were from the beginning eager supporters of the House of Han- over—" among the chief bulwarks of the throne " one of their own historians calls them.[7] Throughout the eighteenth century they remained loyal, while not a few Anglicans sulked or flirted with gentlemen over the water. Circumstances had strangely changed since charges of

[6] Wilson, *Dissenting Churches of London*, 1808, III, pp. 513-14.
[7] H. W. Clark, *op. cit.*, II, p. 180. Cf. Lincoln, *op. cit.*, p. 23.

treason were hurled promiscuously at Dissenters. Nonconformists knew that the maintenance of such liberties as they
and the country generally enjoyed depended on the Hanoverians, and both George I and George II recognized the
advantages of the support they gave.

Its unwavering attitude to the House of Hanover, though
dictated primarily by self-interest, was not the least of Nonconformity's services to England. The Whig Party, which
provided most of the ministries of the time, needed as many
allies as possible. This was the period which saw the
development of our system of cabinet government and the
emergence of the office of Prime Minister.[8] Nonconformists
hoped again and again for relief from the Corporation and
Test Acts and from the payment of tithes, but though their
status in the country greatly improved, no one was willing
to risk the storm which ameliorative proposals would have
roused from the Tories and Churchmen in rural England,
then the chief home of reaction.[9] Nevertheless, Nonconformity did not go unrewarded. In an endeavour to keep
them from making awkward demands, and to show that
their help was appreciated, Walpole arranged in 1723 that
a half-yearly grant should be made from the royal purse " for
the use and behalf of the poor widows of dissenting
ministers ". The fund was to be administered by representatives of the Presbyterians and Independents. There were
certain precedents for this royal gift, but it offended the
consciences of the more radical, particularly as the years
passed. At long last, in 1851, in deference to Nonconformist
appeals, the " Regium Donum ", as it was called, was dis-
continued.

[8] Cf. Trevelyan, *op. cit.*, p. 501.
[9] e.g. the Vicar of Kingsthorpe, Northants, who spoke always of
" the Duke of Brunswick, commonly called King George II ", and
tried to suppress Doddridge's Academy in 1732.

Not the least of the services of Dissenters to the House of Hanover was their staunchness at the time of the rebellion of the Young Pretender. Led by Doddridge, ministers in many parts encouraged the raising of volunteers, and even the Quakers collected flannels for the troops. A special Act indemnifying Dissenters for breaking the Test Act by accepting commissions in the Army was afterwards passed, and an annual act gave relief to any who through ignorance or accident failed to carry out the provisions of the Corporation and Test Acts. This annual measure which was continued from 1727 to 1828, when the objectionable Acts at last disappeared from the statute book, followed the organization of the Presbyterian, Congregational and Baptist ministers of London into the " Three Denominations ", a formally organized body which marked an important step in the consolidation of Dissent. Five years later, in 1732, a committee was set up known as the " Dissenting Deputies ". This brought together laymen as well as ministers from all churches within ten miles of London to defend and extend the civil rights of Dissenters. Their struggle was to be a long one. But one minor episode may here be mentioned, one that occupied the years from 1748 to 1767. The Corporation of the City of London imposed heavy fines on those who refused the office of Sheriff. Under the Corporation Act only one who took communion at the parish church could hold office. There is abundant evidence that Nonconformists were deliberately elected that their fines might go towards the cost of the new Mansion House. Long years of litigation were necessary before Lord Chief Justice Mansfield ruled that Nonconformists had the right to decline to serve.

Co-operation in the struggle for civil rights was accompanied by much theological discussion, the effects of which showed themselves increasingly after 1719, the date of a " synod " at Salter's Hall when London ministers were faced with difficult decisions about a case referred to them from Exeter.[10]   Three Presbyterian ministers were there suspected of heterodox views on the Trinity and the Person of Christ.   The suggestion that the members of the London gathering should subscribe to the first of the Anglican Articles of Religion and the fifth and sixth questions of the Shorter Westminster Catechism at once divided the company and raised two issues of considerable importance, not before seriously faced by Protestants: first, the nature of the authority of the ancient symbols of the Catholic Church, and the relation of the New Testament thereto, and, secondly, the subject of individual liberty of opinion in matters of religion.   The details of the Salter's Hall Synod are not very edifying.   It registered and precipitated a considerable swing towards Socinian and Unitarian views, in all three denominations, particularly among the Presbyterians.   But the controversies which resulted have been of continuing importance both because of the theological issues involved and because the question of the meaning of subscription to creeds and formularies and the limits of private judgment are not even yet finally settled.

Dr. F. J. Powicke argues vigorously and effectively that three things commonly asserted of the outcome of the Salter's Hall Synod are not true.[11]   It is not true that the Presbyterian ministers alleged to be Arian were, as a rule, less evangelistic than the orthodox Independents; nor that alleged Arians were to blame for emphasizing the moral side of Christianity—this was indeed their glory; nor that Presbyterian churches, said to be tainted by Arianism, withered away under its influence.   So far as these charges have

---

[10] For a full account see A. Gordon, *Addresses Biographical and Historical*, 1922.

[11] *Essays Congregational and Catholic*, pp. 306f.   Cf. O. M. Griffiths, *Religion and Learning*, 1935.

truth in them they represent tendencies at work in all the churches, and in the Church of England as well as the Dissenting bodies. Things were none too healthy in the religious life of England. "The most depressing twenty years in English Christianity in the eighteenth century were those between 1730 and 1750," says J. H. Colligan.[12] Yet it is important to note that during that period from the Church of England there came William Law's *Serious Call to a Devout and Holy Life* and Bishop Butler's *Analogy of Religion*,[13] both of them works that continue influential, and that from Nonconformity there came the hymns of Isaac Watts and Philip Doddridge. Moreover, it was during the same period that the Wesleys and Whitefield were prepared for their mighty work.

III

Watts and Doddridge[14] deserve special mention, for their hymns have become an integral part of the English religious heritage and have been adopted by the whole Christian Church. The two men may be taken as representatives worthy to stand beside any contemporary religious leaders.

[12] *Eighteenth-Century Nonconformity*, 1915, p. 90. Piette, *John Wesley in the Evolution of Protestantism*, 1937, pp. 110f., illustrates "the frightful seepage in English moral life" during this period. R. F. Wearmouth, *Methodism and the Common People of the Eighteenth Century*, 1945, gives details of the disorders and distress and of the effect of the penal system. Duncan Coomer, *English Dissent under the Early Hanoverians*, 1946, describes the life of the churches and their first contacts with Methodism.

[13] Law, it may further be noted, was under Quaker influence (see Stephen Hobhouse, *William Law and Eighteenth-Century Quakerism*, 1927); Butler was educated at a Dissenting Academy.

[14] Thomas Milner, *The Life, Times and Correspondence of Isaac Watts*, 1834, throws much light on the Dissent of the period. An English edition of a useful American study of Watts by A. P. Davis was published in 1948. On his hymns see Bernard Manning, *The Hymns of Watts and Wesley*, 1942. For Doddridge, Charles Stanford, *Philip Doddridge*, 1880, remains an excellent introduction.

Isaac Watts, who was born in 1674 in Southampton, came of Dissenting stock. His father was a schoolmaster and deacon of a congregation which had as its minister one who had been ejected in 1662. Watts, senior, suffered imprisonment for his convictions during the later years of Charles II, and for two years, when his son was quite small, lived quietly in London to escape the attention of the authorities. Isaac was a serious child with an early taste for verse-making, apparently inherited from his father. In 1690 he left the local grammar school, where he had had a grounding in Latin, Greek, French and Hebrew, and went to the Dissenting Academy at Stoke Newington to train for the ministry. Defoe had been there a decade earlier, and had had Samuel Wesley as a fellow pupil. Isaac Watts was at the Academy for four years, and being then only twenty, returned home for a time. He then went as tutor to the Hartopp family. Sir John, the third baronet, had been a Member of Parliament, and a close friend of John Owen, and had suffered considerably for his Nonconformist convictions. Watts was soon preaching regularly to the Mark Lane congregation which Owen had gathered about him in his last years, and in 1702 became its minister, a position he held till his death forty-six years later.

The early years of Watts's ministry covered the reign of Anne, that time of uncertainty for Dissenters. Lady Abney, wife of Sir Thomas Abney, Lord Mayor of London, and M.P. for the city, was one of Watts's congregation. It was Sir Thomas's " occasional conformity " that provoked Defoe's strictures. Watts lodged for a time with Thomas Hollis, a wealthy Baptist merchant, who—in the Bunyan

There is also J. D. Humphreys, *The Correspondence and Diary of Philip Doddridge*, 5 vols., 1829-31. J. Fergusson, *John Fergusson, 1727-50*, 1948, gives interesting details of one of Doddridge's pupils and some new letters.

tradition—was a member of the Independent church at Pinner's Hall; but, in 1713 or thereabouts, after a serious breakdown in health, he went to live with the Abneys at their homes in Stoke Newington and in Hertfordshire. He remained with them for the rest of his life. He had already become well known for his verses and hymns, *Horae Lyricae* appearing in 1706 and his other most important collections between then and 1719. His theological treatises, which appeared during his later years, showed him as one of the more liberal thinkers of Nonconformity, a moderate Calvinist, having some sympathies with Arianism. He published also a large number of educational manuals.

Slight of stature and always frail, Watts moved in a distinguished circle and gained its respect. He is said to have been, with Matthew Prior, the poet, one of the many unsuccessful suitors for the hand of Elizabeth Singer (Mrs. Thomas Rowe) whose poems gained the enthusiastic praise of Johnson. He was well enough known to find his name included in an early edition of Pope's *Dunciad* and apparently got it removed by a personal remonstrance.[15]

During the reign of George II, relations between Anglicans and Dissenters somewhat improved and Watts had friendly contacts with certain of the bishops. By the time of his death in 1748, although kept from much public activity by severe ill-health, he had become something of a national figure and, though buried in Bunhill Fields, was granted a memorial in Westminster Abbey. He had lived to see the beginnings of the Great Awakening in America and the Methodist Movement in England. He had witnessed the failure of the '45 rebellion and the final collapse of the hopes of those who wished to overthrow the House of Hanover.

It is the hymns of Watts and his metrical versions of the

---

[15] Milner, *op. cit.*, pp. 297, 435-6. Cf. William Cowper's letter to John Newton, September 18th, 1781.

Psalms that are his chief legacy. Many of them were first written for his father's congregation in Southampton. Some of his verses seem to us to-day little better than doggerel, but among them are masterpieces that continue to express the religious emotions of ever-widening circles of Christians. "Our God, our help in ages past", "Jesus shall reign, where'er the sun", and his greatest and possibly best-known composition, "When I survey the wondrous Cross"—these are now part of our common English heritage, part of the heritage of the whole Christian Church. In many of his verses Watts shows himself a typical eighteenth-century Dissenter. His patriotic loyalty to William III and George I finds expression in the application of Psalm seventy-five to his native land.

> " Britain was doom'd to be a slave
> Her frame dissolv'd, her fears were great
> When God a new supporter gave
> To bear the pillars of the State.
>
> He from Thy hand receiv'd his crown,
> And swore to rule by wholesome laws;
> His foot shall tread th' oppressor down,
> His arm defend the righteous cause."

Watts's religious thought has a cosmic background and a delight in Nature which, as Bernard Manning observes, he may well owe, like his flair for the memorable phrase, and his masterly use of proper names, to Milton. His vocabulary is pure Anglo-Saxon like that of Bunyan. But his work lives because he deals with " the great common themes of catholic Christianity ", and because the notes of simplicity and sincerity are continually sounded. Here again is Nonconformity showing its truly English, but also its truly universal quality.

F

In his later years Watts took an eager interest in the work of Philip Doddridge, his junior by twenty-eight years. Doddridge was a notable and attractive figure. His mother was the daughter of a refugee from Bohemia, who brought with him few possessions save a treasured copy of Luther's translation of the German Bible. His father came of an old and distinguished West Country family which had only reluctantly taken the Parliamentary side in the seventeenth century. After the early death of his father and mother, young Doddridge found himself at St. Albans and there, at the age of sixteen, joined an Independent church and turned his thoughts towards the ministry. Tempting offers were made to send him to Oxford if he would conform. Calamy, depressed by the decline in the strength of Nonconformity and by its restrictions, advised him to choose some other career. But his St. Albans friends helped the young man to an academy at Kibworth, where he made good use of his time. At the age of twenty-three he was minister in Market Harborough, able and charming, fond of society, male and female, and sought after in many parts of the country. When only twenty-seven he was chosen by his brethren to be the head of a new academy and shortly afterwards moved to Northampton, which was to be the centre of his activities for the remaining twenty years of his relatively brief life.

Doddridge is notable for his services to ministerial education, for the readiness with which he welcomed the early signs of religious revival, for his strong social sympathies, witnessed to particularly by his part in the founding of Northampton hospital, for his attempts to promote interest in missionary work,[16] and for his desire for the widest Christian fellowship and understanding. He was an eager supporter of the House of Hanover, and in 1745 took a

[16] See E. A. Payne, *Before the Start: Steps Towards the Founding of the L.M.S.*, 1942, pp. 5f.

leading part in organizing local resistance to the Pretender.
It was after this that he had discussions with one or two
bishops about the healing of the breach between the Anglican Church and Dissenters, and proposed some kind of
mutual recognition of orders. " Yet," as he wrote in 1748,
" I am so thoroughly persuaded of the reasonableness of
Nonconformity, and find so many of the terms of ministerial
conformity contrary to the dictates of my conscience in the
sight of God, that I was never less inclined to submit to
them. I hope I shall not be willing to buy my liberty or life
at that price. But I think it my duty to do my part towards
promoting that mutual peace and goodwill which I think
more likely than anything else, either to reform the Church,
or else to promote true Christianity both in the Establishment and separation; to strengthen the Protestant cause, and
to defeat the designs of our common enemies."[17] Doddridge's writings were of considerable importance in his own
generation and for some time subsequently, particularly his
Family Expositor, which enables his biographer to claim
for him " the honour of being the first who attempted to
popularize a critical knowledge of the Bible ",[18] and the
Rise and Progress of Religion in the Soul. The latter was
undertaken with Watts's encouragement and had remarkable success as a guide to personal religion, as its influence
on William Wilberforce, on Carey's friend, Samuel Pearce,
and, two generations later, on Alexander McLaren may
testify.

There remain Doddridge's hymns. He had not the
facility of Watts, but not a few of his compositions have won
a permanent place in the worship of many different branches
of the Church. " Hark! the glad sound, the Saviour
comes ", " O God of Bethel, by whose hand Thy people still

---

[17] Stanford, *op. cit.*, p. 156.
[18] *Ibid.*, p. 162.

are fed ", and " O happy day, that fixed my choice " tell of a warm personal religion and still speak to the heart.

IV

It will be convenient here to say a further word or so about the Dissenting academies. They represent a contribution to English education the importance of which is increasingly recognized. The earliest came into existence immediately after the Act of Uniformity of 1662. Their main aim was the training of ministers, since Oxford and Cambridge were closed to Dissenters, but increasingly they opened their doors to the sons of Dissenters whatever career was intended. They rapidly made a position for themselves as is proved by the spiteful and all but successful attacks made upon them during the reign of Queen Anne. Some of the most learned of the ejected clergy gave themselves to the work of teaching, and having more freedom than the ancient universities, the academies developed a curriculum which, whilst it did not neglect the classics, had a place for the newly developing interest in mathematics and science.

Reference has already been made to the Academy at Stoke Newington which was attended by Samuel Wesley and Daniel Defoe, and later by Isaac Watts. Its first head was Charles Morton whose " chiefest excellence lay in Mathematics, and especially the mechanical part of them ". Early in the reign of James II, persecution by the unfriendly authorities drove him to New England where he became Vice-President of Harvard College, an institution greatly benefited by Morton's successor at Newington, the learned Theophilus Gale, and a generation later by Thomas Hollis, junior. But the Newington Academy was only one among many. Miss Parker[19] lists nearly two dozen founded before

[19] *Dissenting Academies in England*, 1914. Cf. H. McLachlan, *English Education under the Test Acts*, 1931; A. Lincoln, *op. cit.*, Ch. III; O. M. Griffiths, *op. cit.*, pp. 35f.

the Revolution of 1688, and more than another thirty between 1690 and 1750. Among their pupils, in addition to those already named, we find Calamy, Matthew Henry, Thomas Secker (afterwards Archbishop of Canterbury), Joseph Butler, and, later, Joseph Priestley. They maintained fruitful contacts with Holland, America and Scotland, and throughout the century formed a striking contrast to the decadent universities of Oxford and Cambridge. In the next generation the academies had an important part in the education of William Godwin, Robert Malthus, John Foster, and William Hazlitt.

Sir Fred Clarke has recently given high praise to the academies for the independent line they took in educational matters. " They were," he says, " less concerned with a code of formal accomplishments distinctive of an aristocratic class and a governing tradition, and much more concerned with the specific attainments necessary for effective living *at their own social level and in their own milieu* in what they knew to be a significantly changing world. We must relate them, therefore, to the Royal Society, to the inventions of the eighteenth century, to the beginnings of the Industrial Revolution and to the modes of thought which gave rise to the revolutions in America and in France."[20] This is high praise, and a further evidence of the important contribution made by Nonconformists to the life of modern England.

[20] *Education and Social Change*, 1940, pp. 15-16. Cf. G. Kitson Clark, *The English Inheritance*, 1950, p. 116 : " In the eighteenth century possibly the best systematic political education that was given in the country was given in the great Dissenting Academies."

CHAPTER FIVE

Revival: Wesley and His Contemporaries

No man lived nearer to the centre than John Wesley, neither Pitt nor Clive, neither Mansfield nor Johnson. You cannot cut him out of the national life. No single figure influenced so many minds, no single voice touched so many hearts. No other man did such a life's work for England.

AUGUSTINE BIRRELL,
Essays and Reviews, p. 15.

THE BIOGRAPHER of Doddridge gives us an attractive picture of his simple meeting-house on Castle Hill, Northampton, and the congregation that gathered there. There was space for about seven hundred persons. The roof was propped by two white wooden pillars. There were galleries, also whitened, and a clumsy white pulpit surmounted by a great sounding board. In front of the pulpit stood a long massive communion-table, at each side of which sat the students of Doddridge's Academy, and over which hung a large brass candlestick with many branches. In the galleries might often be seen men of the dragoons. In not a few of the deep square pews downstairs were important personages—ladies of the family of the Duke of Bedford, sometimes the great-grandson of Oliver Cromwell, and often the stately Colonel Gardiner, who had been wounded at the battle of Blenheim and converted after a dissolute life, and who was to die a heroic death at Prestonpans in 1745 (the same Colonel Gardiner whose life, written by Doddridge, created something of a sensation, and who may also be found in the pages of Scott's *Waverley*). But most of the congregation was made up of small gentry, shopkeepers, farmers from the country, farm labourers and many of the poorer classes in the town. Doddridge preached in a long white wig and a dark blue Geneva gown, and on stepping into the pulpit hung his triangular hat on the peg behind him. For some years the singing of the Psalms was to the accompaniment of flutes and fiddles. Later these were done away with and the clerk took the lead. At the close of the sermon a hymn—often a new composition of the preacher's —was given out line by line and sung. After morning worship those of the congregation who had come in from the country brought out their dinners. Then Doddridge catechized the children. The second service was in the afternoon. Once a month, when the moon was full, the Lord's Supper was celebrated. Otherwise there was not usually an evening service, the bad roads and the darkness making it too difficult to assemble.[1]

For most of the twenty years of Doddridge's ministry the church prospered and was at peace. It may be taken as a representative of the best that Nonconformity achieved in those days. Not long before the honoured pastor died, however, there were serious internal dissensions over those who favoured Moravianism.[2] And, unfortunately, we can-

[1] See Stanford, *op. cit.*, Ch. X. Horton Davies, *The Worship of the English Puritans*, 1948, provides a valuable study of the Puritan tradition of worship from the days of Cranmer to Watts.

[2] Religious refugees from Moravia found asylum early in the eighteenth century on the estates of Count Zinzendorf in Saxony. Their piety and missionary zeal made a deep impression. Through the visits to England of certain of their missionaries and Zinzendorf himself, and the evangelistic work of Benjamin Ingham and John Cennick, a number of English Moravian congregations were formed from 1738 onwards. In 1749 the British Moravian Church received

not take Doddridge's church as typical of the Nonconformity of the period. Not many minutes' walk away, in Northampton, were three or four other groups, of no great size, which spent much of their time in quarrels involving the trustees of their properties and in disputings over theological matters and over the disciplining of their members for marriage with unbelievers, intemperance, immorality, bankruptcy, going to the Quakers' meeting, and the like.[3] Anyone who has turned the pages of eighteenth-century minute-books knows how narrow and introspective many Dissenting churches had become, how fine the doctrinal hair-splitting over the various types of Calvinism in some, in others how arid the rationalizing regarding the Trinity and the person of Christ. In the West Country many of the Presbyterian and General Baptist churches had become sympathetic with Arianism. Others were infected with a dangerous repudiation of all moral restraints in the supposed interests of grace. Almost everywhere enthusiasm was at a discount and there was little aggressive work.

Yet large numbers of people were quite untouched by religion. They were poor, illiterate, uncared for. The Established Church was in a sorry state also—" apathetic, sceptical, lifeless ", says Halévy, giving details of the political jobbery that governed preferment, the nepotism, the pluralities, the scandalously low level of spiritual life among the clergy which disgraced the age. " The churches actually in existence were empty," he says, " and a clergy devoid of conscientiousness or zeal had an interest in their remaining

Parliamentary recognition. See W. G. Addison, *The Renewed Church of the United Brethren, 1722-1930*, 1932.

[3] See John Taylor, *The Bicentenary of College Street Church, Northampton*, 1897, pp. 14-22, but note again church covenants which provide for " difference of opinion about water Baptism " and where the main emphasis is on life rather than doctrine.

empty."[4] Such was the situation when a great new spiritual impulse made itself felt and the Evangelical Revival began, a revival which changed the face of England, which brought new vigour and power to all the existing branches of the Church and created new ones, sending out influences into all spheres of life and, ultimately, to all parts of the world.

Spiritual origins are extremely elusive. " The wind bloweth where it listeth." The outstanding human agent in what happened in this country was John Wesley, an Anglican priest, but beside him was his brother, Charles, and George Whitefield, and Selina, Countess of Huntingdon, and a host of others, who under their inspiration became preachers and evangelists. Moreover, the Wesleys and Whitefield, though associated while at Oxford in the " Holy Club.", wherein they sought by strict method to discipline and develop their own spirituality, were not launched on the great work of their lives until they had had contact with other sources of new zeal and power, the Wesleys with the Moravians, and Whitefield with a movement in New England which owed its origin to the labours of Jonathan Edwards. This last—the so-called Great Awakening—first showed itself in 1735, thus antedating the revival in this country. In *The Preacher*, Whittier describes vividly how :

" In the church of the wilderness Edwards wrought,
Shaping his creed at the forge of thought;
And with Thor's own hammer welded and bent
The iron links of his argument,
Which strove to grasp in its mighty span
The purpose of God and the fate of man ! "

and then, as at last in answer to his prayers, a quickening of spiritual life showed itself among his people,

[4] *Op. cit.*, Bk. III, Ch. 1. Cf. Piette, *op. cit.*, Bk. II.

"Lo! by the Merrimack WHITEFIELD stands."

Further, when young Whitefield visited Scotland in 1741, just after returning from America, he found a remarkable religious quickening taking place in the Cambuslang neighbourhood—of apparently quite independent origin. One discovers strange links between individuals and groups in widely separated places. Just as a century earlier young George Fox discovered little companies of "seekers" in the North of England, so in different parts of a Britain that seemed religiously spent and lifeless there were those who were prayerfully waiting for the consolation of Israel and who did not wait in vain.

II

John Wesley[5] was born in 1703 in the rectory of Epworth, Lincolnshire. His mother—and John was emphatically the son of his mother, he was the fifteenth child and second surviving son—was a daughter of the Presbyterian, Samuel Annesley, under whose ministry Defoe grew up. His father was educated at the Newington Academy for the Independent ministry and was Defoe's contemporary there; he conformed in order to enter Exeter College, Oxford, moved perhaps partly by growing doubts about Dissenting principles, partly by personal ambition and partly by the overconfident expectation of John Owen, then in his last years,

---

[5] Wesley's own *Journal*, the classic account of his activities, may be had in the Everyman Library (4 vols.). It has been effectively abridged and edited by Nora Ratcliff, 1940. Of the many modern studies of Wesley and the Revival, see the volumes by J. S. Simon, 1921-27, Maldwyn Edwards, *John Wesley and the Eighteenth Century*, 1933, Croft Cell, *The Rediscovery of Wesley*, 1935, and M. Piette, *John Wesley in the Evolution of Protestantism*, 1926 (E.T. 1937). Quiller-Couch, *Hetty Wesley*, Marjorie Bowen, *Wrestling Jacob* and G. Harrison, *Son to Susanna* are imaginative reconstructions.

that degrees in Oxford would soon be open to Nonconformists. Whatever the reasons, he soon became a most
ardent Churchman, and in 1703 there was published an
attack upon the inner life of Dissenting academies which he
had written privately some years before. Mrs. Wesley had
at one time favoured Socinian views and was brought back
to orthodoxy by her husband's influence; she was a remarkable woman, ready on occasion to supply the deficiencies of
the Epworth curates and to read prayers and a sermon to
her family and as many as two hundred neighbours. John
Wesley was brought up a strict Anglican. He claimed to
be a loyal son of the Church to the day of his death. But
it cannot be gainsaid that Puritanism and Restoration Nonconformity were a part of his personal heritage.

After their training at Oxford, John and his brother,
Charles—two intense young men, already " Methodists " in
their spiritual routine and most eager to do good to their
fellows—set out for Georgia under the auspices of the Society
for the Propagation of the Gospel, which sent out Anglican
chaplains to the colonists. On the voyage, and out in
Georgia, they were in close touch with Moravians, whose
piety and zeal deeply impressed them. Shortly after their
return to England (due largely to personal indiscretions)
they both, at meetings of a Moravian society in Aldersgate
Street, passed through an evangelical experience which they
described as their " conversion ". Wesley's own account of
what happened to him on May 24th, 1738, has become
historic. " In the evening I went very unwillingly to a
society in Aldersgate-street, where one was reading Luther's
preface to the Epistle to the Romans. About a quarter
before nine, while he was describing the change which God
works in the heart through faith in Christ, I felt my heart
strangely warmed. I felt I did trust in Christ, Christ alone,
for salvation; and an assurance was given me, that he had

taken away *my* sins, even *mine*, and saved *me* from the law
of sin and death." What this experience meant to John and
his brother can perhaps best be appreciated from the triumphant hymn which Charles wrote in the first ardour of his
new enthusiasm: " O for a thousand tongues to sing my
great Redeemer's praise."

> " Jesus! the name that charms our fears,
>   That bids our sorrows cease;
> 'Tis music in the sinner's ears,
>   'Tis life, and health, and peace.
>
> He breaks the power of cancelled sin,
>   He sets the prisoner free;
> His blood can make the foulest clean,
>   His blood availed for me.
>
> Look unto Him, ye nations, own
>   Your God, ye fallen race;
> Look, and be saved through faith alone,
>   Be justified by grace."

George Whitefield, their Oxford friend, had already revealed
great gifts as a popular preacher, and, cutting through the
current ecclesiastical formality and red tape, began the novel
practice of open-air preaching at Kingswood Hill, near
Bristol, in February, 1739. Three months later, aglow with
the desire to proclaim to men the good news of personal
salvation by faith, Wesley did likewise and established in
Bristol a " New Room " in which members of the religious
societies he proposed to form could meet. Within a very
short time, in spite of official reprobation and opposition, the
Wesleys and Whitefield were going up and down the land,
preaching wherever they could, in private buildings and
meeting-houses, occasionally in parish churches, if the in-

cumbents would allow them, more often in the fields and market-places. Crowds flocked to hear them.

Wesley was an Arminian in theology, Whitefield (probably under the influence of Jonathan Edwards) a Calvinist. The effects of their preaching were not very different. Much religious excitement and controversy were aroused. Wesley soon demonstrated his outstanding gifts as an organizer. His own work and that of his associates was at first intended to be merely supplementary to the ordinary services of the Church. He was led on step by step, largely by the opposition he met in official quarters, to develop an organization which in the end became a separate body and one of the Free Churches. Wesley's overmastering concern was that the gospel should be preached. He believed that those who had once responded to the message should be nurtured in the faith. A sufficient number of sympathetic clergymen not being available, he enlisted the aid of lay evangelists. In 1760 these began to administer the sacraments, and in 1784 Wesley set apart Thomas Coke as " superintendent " of a mission to America and " ordained " two " presbyters " to assist him. Shortly afterwards he " ordained " men for work in Scotland, and in 1787 he registered his chapels and preachers under the Toleration Act. These steps, forced upon him as they were, led inevitably to a complete breach with the Church of England, which was not able to adapt itself to the freedom of his methods.

Short and slim, a dauntless figure, for half a century he travelled the length and breadth of England on horseback, covering, it is said, 250,000 miles, reading as he rode, talking to all he met, preaching here, there, and everywhere, to all sorts and conditions of men—" never at leisure ", as Johnson once complained to Boswell. The years of his activity were those of the Seven Years' War with France and of the war of American Independence. Wesley had strong views on politics, of a generally Tory type. He was interested in medicine and education, in orphanages and Sunday Schools, in the early protests against the slave-trade. Indeed, just as he claimed to take the world as his parish, so he could say that no human interest was alien to him; but his main concern to the very end of his long life was the presentation to as many people as possible of the challenge to vital, inward religion.

At the time of Wesley's death in 1791 there were in Britain some sixty thousand members of Methodist societies, together with many more adherents,[6] but it is not by figures like these that his influence can be assessed, for, in addition, throughout the older Dissenting bodies and in a section of the Anglican Church, his message was at work. Moreover, side by side with the Methodists was the small but not insignificant group known as the Countess of Huntingdon's Connexion, another offshoot of the revival, and the result of the work of one of the most remarkable women of the century, who early threw in her lot with the Methodists and Evangelicals.[7]

Methodism was destined to be far more than a transient quickening or renewal of spiritual life. It continued to grow in strength and, as we shall have cause to note hereafter, has made a most important contribution to modern England in many different directions. Wesley's figure has continued an inspiration to succeeding generations. He is from that point of view unique. As a nation we are not given to hero-worship. No other of our outstanding religious personalities

[6] Maldwyn Edwards, *After Wesley*, 1935, p. 143. R. F. Wearmouth, *op. cit.*, p. 176, reckons 120,000 members in Britain and America, with four times as many attending Methodist preaching.

[7] There is, unfortunately, no modern biography of the Countess. *The Life and Times of Selina, Countess of Huntingdon*, 2 vols., 1839-40, is a confused agglomeration of material.

remains vital and authoritative in quite the same way as does Wesley. The reason for this lies largely in the man himself. He was one who—to borrow the words of Bernard Manning—" by a stroke of divine genius that puts him in the same rank as Hildebrand, St. Dominic, and St. Ignatius Loyola, combined the evangelical passion and experience of Luther with Calvin's ecclesiastical system ". " The unique strength of Methodism," he continues, " comes from its marvellous use of both the new creative forces in modern religion."[8]

One of the more immediate and personal legacies of Wesley was the hymn book he edited, but to which his brother Charles was the main and outstanding contributor. It first appeared in 1780, and in the preface Wesley claimed it as " a body of practical and experimental divinity ". It is that and more. In the Free Churches a hymn book takes the place occupied by the Prayer Book in the devotional life, public and private, of the Anglican. This in part explains how it is that the hymns of Watts, Doddridge and the Wesleys have so entered into the life of the English people. John Wesley's own best hymns were translations from the German. Charles had an original gift of unsurpassed range and effectiveness, and in simple, direct, but moving and memorable verse, he set forth " not the amiable generalizations of natural religion in which Wesley's contemporaries delighted, but the peculiar and pungent doctrines of uncompromising Christianity ".[9] He is said to have written more than six thousand hymns. " Come, O Thou Traveller unknown " is a religious poem rather than a hymn, identifying

[8] *The Making of Modern English Religion*, 1929, pp. 109-10.
[9] Manning, *The Hymns of Wesley and Watts*, 1942, p. 27. Cf. J. E. Rattenbury, *The Evangelical Doctrines of Charles Wesley's Hymns*, 1941, *The Eucharistic Hymns of John and Charles Wesley*, 1948, and George Sampson, *A Century of Divine Songs*, 1943, pp. 12-23.

wrestling Jacob with the soul of man. It was written in 1742, and so moved Isaac Watts that he said it was worth all the verses he had written. Open any modern hymnal, belonging to almost any of the main branches of the Church, and one may see the debt Christendom owes to Charles Wesley. "Hark! the herald angels sing", "Christ the Lord is risen to-day", "Jesus, Lover of my soul", "Soldiers of Christ, arise", "Gentle Jesus, meek and mild"—these are but a few of the more famous. It was hymns like these that helped to spread the evangelical message and to make religion real again to tens of thousands of men and women.

III

Most of the Dissenters of the old type were somewhat suspicious of John Wesley, and he of them. As we have seen, they had become infected with the spirit of the age and shared the general distrust of enthusiasm. Wesley was an Anglican clergyman, and to the very end repudiated connections with Dissenters as such. He was an Arminian; most of them were Calvinists, of one kind or another. He was a Tory; most of them were Whigs, if not—at any rate in George III's reign—republicans. Occasionally, a Nonconformist minister would open his meeting-house for Wesley to preach in,[10] but it did not often happen, and in the main the term "Methodist" was one of abuse on the lips of Dissenters. With the Calvinistic George Whitefield —a man who sat far more loosely to ecclesiastical tradition— Dissenters found it far easier to have fellowship, and on his preaching journeys throughout England, Scotland and Wales, and at his chapel in Tottenham Court Road and his tabernacle in Bristol he was often in contact with them.

The influence of revival on Dissent may be seen in three

[10] e.g. in Towcester on November 25th, 1789.

other directions: first, in certain largely independent stir-
rings, secondly, in the work of Dan Taylor among the
General Baptists, and thirdly, in the impulses which came
from contacts between certain Dissenters and evangelical
Anglicans. The writings of Jonathan Edwards and the
account of the " Great Awakening " in New England had
a powerful effect on the narrow hyper-Calvinism of many
Nonconformists. Edwards's life of the saintly young David
Brainerd and accounts of the latter's work among the Red
Indians reached this country in time for Doddridge to be
stirred by them.[11] The book exercised a wide influence.
The fruitful evangelistic ministries of men like Doddridge's
one-time pupil, Risdon Darracott, in the West Country
between 1741 and 1759, or of Baptist pastors like Benjamin
Beddome who was at Bourton-on-the-Water from 1740-95,
or Daniel Turner, who was at Abingdon from 1748-98,
cannot be ascribed either to the Wesleys or to George Whitefield. Nor can the powerful forces at work in the mind of
young Andrew Fuller leading to his book *The Gospel
Worthy of All Acceptation* (1785), which challenged Nonconformity over a wide area of the Midlands and beyond,
and played its part in making Baptists ready to hear the call
to foreign missions.

By the middle of the eighteenth century the General Baptists were largely Socinian in theology and in a very low
state spiritually. Through the zeal of Dan Taylor, the son
of a Yorkshire miner, who had been influenced first by
Methodists, and who afterwards came to Baptist convictions,
a New Connexion was formed among them, which quickly
showed signs of vigorous life. At the beginning of his
career, while a schoolmaster and preacher in Wadsworth,
Taylor had the help of a young man named Sutcliff, who,
after training at the one Baptist Academy, Bristol, arrived

[11] J. D. Humphreys, *op. cit.*, V., pp. 171, 189, etc.

G

in 1775 in Olney. There the Anglican curate was the famous John Newton, who had at one time engaged in the African slave-trade and whose strong religious impressions had been deepened under the influence of Whitefield and Wesley. The sensitive William Cowper had settled in Olney in 1767 and a few years later he and Newton produced the *Olney Hymns*. In this quiet Buckinghamshire town during the seventies and eighties the closest fellowship existed between Anglicans and Dissenters, a fellowship prophetic of that which was to be seen a generation later when evangelicals of all parties joined in the formation of the Bible Society and kindred organizations.

To the same period belongs the rousing of Wales and the establishment of the Calvinistic Methodist Church, for the main work was done between 1736 and 1773. Its fruit may be seen in the overwhelmingly Nonconformist character of modern Welsh religion. The chief agent was Howel Harris, born on a Breconshire farm, who, eager to enter the established Church, went down from Oxford after less than a week there in 1735 and began ardent evangelistic work, which soon brought him into conflict with the ecclesiastical authorities. He was refused ordination, but, like Wesley, regarded himself as a loyal member of the Anglican Church. Wesley once declared that the Welsh were " as little versed in the principles of Christianity as a Creek or a Cherokee Indian ".[12] This is somewhat exaggerated, but there is no doubt at all as to the generally lamentable condition of things. Such Nonconformity as there was was confined almost entirely to South Wales, and within that, as in England, there were tendencies to Socinianism.[13]

[12] Quoted by Silvester Horne, *op. cit.*, p. 304. Cf. M. G. Jones, *The Charity School Movement*, 1938, Ch. VIII.

[13] For earlier Puritanism and Nonconformity in Wales see Thomas Rees, *Protestant Nonconformity in Wales*, 1861, and Thomas Richards, *The Puritan Movement in Wales, 1639-1653*, 1920, *Reli-*

Within six or seven years, Howel Harris, a young clergy-man named Daniel Rowlands, and William Williams, of Pantycelyn, had roused the whole Principality, though often at great personal danger. Whitefield gave them every en-couragement, but the movement in Wales was parallel to, rather than the result of, the revival in England. Harris is described as commanding in appearance, and as possessing a quite irresistible earnestness. His elder brother, Joseph, had become assay-master of the mint and an important authority on currency questions. In his later years, influenced by what the Pietists had done in Halle and Whitefield in his Orphan House in Georgia, Howel established a religious community in his native Trevecca. Then, when he feared a French invasion, he joined the militia, preaching more than once in England in his regimental dress, and becoming a close friend of the Countess of Huntingdon who founded a College for ministers in Trevecca. The Welsh Calvinistic Methodists were generally Presbyterian in polity. Only gradually, and in spite of themselves, did they come to com-plete separation from the Anglican Church. The new religious enthusiasm soon passed into the Independent and Baptist bodies in Wales, and they also began rapidly to increase.

So in one place after another, now here, now there, the tokens of revival were seen, foreshadowing the period of unparalleled evangelistic expansion which was shortly to follow.

IV

Yet to complete the picture of Nonconformity as it was during the age of Wesley, we have to note two other groups, the Unitarians and the Quakers, both of whom remained

gious Development in Wales, 1654-1662, 1923, and Wales under the Penal Code, 1662-1687, 1925.

largely unaffected by the revival movement. In spite of this, both made important contributions to the evolution of modern England.

The growth of Arian and Socinian ideas in the eighteenth century has already been noticed. As these labels have often been wildly and abusively used, it is perhaps better to speak of the increasing tendency to question the principle of subscription to the ancient creeds and formularies, and to study both the New Testament and the history and doctrines of the Church from a critical standpoint. This tendency was to be found within the Church of England as well as in all the Dissenting bodies. Of the latter, the Presbyterians and the General Baptists were those most affected. A great impetus to the movement was given by the life and work of Joseph Priestley, but it was an Anglican clergyman, Theophilus Lindsey, who, in 1773, after the failure of a petition to Parliament for some relaxation in the terms of subscription, resigned his living, and, shortly afterwards, opened in Essex Street, Strand, a Unitarian chapel and thus "first organized Unitarian Dissent as a working force in the religious life of England ".[14] Seventeen years later Lindsey, Priestley and Belsham founded the Unitarian Society, the basis of which was an assertion of the unity of

[14] Quoted in *Encyclopedia of Religion and Ethics*, XII, p. 523. Cf. R. V. Holt, *The Unitarian Contribution to Social Progress in England*, 1938, p. 287. H. W. Clark, *op. cit.*, II, p. 310, may be quoted for its tribute, though a rather condescending one, to Lindsey and his associates, and as an illustration of the general attitude of the older Nonconformist bodies towards the Unitarians: " Belsham, Lindsey, Aspland and Toulmin are names which confer lustre on any denomination's story and while all these men were of highest character, Lindsey showed, as another Unitarian, Martineau, was to show after him, that if Unitarianism is scarcely likely to produce saintliness by its own positive force, saints can at any rate find shelter beneath its wing." But a strong case can be made out for the claim of Miller and Johnson, *The Puritans*, p. 4: " Unitarianism is as much the child of Puritanism as Methodism."

God and the simple humanity of Jesus Christ, in opposition both to the orthodox Trinitarian formulae and to ancient Arian teaching.

Priestley's main work was then already done. He was a remarkable man, sharing many traits of character with his famous contemporary John Wesley. Of Yorkshire birth, he came, in 1751, to the Dissenting Academy of which Doddridge had been the distinguished head and which, on the latter's death, was moved to Daventry. Already as a student he found a sterile orthodoxy unsatisfactory and began a free and candid examination of all religious questions. A hereditary stammer kept him from being much of a success in the pulpit, but his vivacity and sincerity won him many friends, and in 1761 he became a tutor at the Warrington Dissenting Academy, moving six years later to a chapel in Leeds. Already he was becoming known for his theological writings, which were all liberal in spirit, and also for the scientific experiments in which he delighted in his spare time. Had he been more orthodox he might have secured appointment as astronomer to Captain Cook's second expedition to the South Seas. From 1772 to 1780 he was librarian to Lord Shelburne, still preaching as a Dissenter, still writing, still experimenting. The name he had made for himself caused him to be offered a Government pension, but this he refused as an ardent Nonconformist and an early protester against the *regium donum*. For the forwarding of his scientific work he relied upon the gifts of private friends. In 1791 his support of the French Revolution and his opposition to Burke, led to an attack by a " Church-and-King " mob upon the Birmingham meeting-house where he had preached since 1780, and his private house, which with all its contents was destroyed. How general was the disapproval of this dastardly attack may be seen, not only from the compensation given him, and the severe punishment of certain of the offenders, but also in the fact that a Baptist chapel, of Calvinistic outlook, opened its pulpit to him a few weeks later. Nevertheless reaction from the terror in Paris caused Priestley to be much maligned in the following years. He lived for a time in London and in 1794 went to America, where he died ten years later, a somewhat pathetic figure. "The Declaration of the Rights of Man in one hand, and the Book of Revelation in the other, Priestley awaited the imminent fall of the Papacy and of the Ottoman Empire and the return of the Jews to Judea."[15] He expected the Second Coming of Christ and the dawn of the Millennium not later than 1814.

It was Cuvier who said that Priestley was "a father of modern Chemistry . . . who would never acknowledge his daughter". His scientific work was but a side-line, yet it was work of the greatest importance. He was one of the earliest of those interested in electricity, and he was the "discoverer" of oxygen. And it was not just chance that these early contributions to modern science should be made by a Nonconformist minister. The tradition in the Dissenting Academies has already been referred to. An eager interest in the world around them, a readiness to experiment, a spirit of candid inquiry characterized the so-called "Rational Dissenters", the greatest of whom was Priestley, and all subsequent generations are their debtors.[16] The same qualities showed themselves in his theological work. Much of it strikes us as somewhat crude and barren. Rightly to estimate it, it must be seen as a brave and candid attempt to apply the same spirit to Scripture and to doctrine.

[15] Lincoln, *op. cit.,* p. 173.
[16] Cf. Gilbert Wakefield, writing in 1792: "These, take them all together, are, in one word, the most respectable set of men I know: genuine lovers of truth, liberty and science." Quoted by Lincoln, *op. cit.,* p. 31. Cf. also the tribute to the Unitarian tradition in America by W. L. Sperry, *op. cit.,* pp. 89f.

From his willingness to be a pioneer, all branches of the Church have benefited, not least those who have rejected his conclusions and treated his name with all but dishonour.

The Rational Dissenters were practically untouched by the Methodist Revival. So also—and this at first seems somewhat strange—were the Quakers. The latter, however, bereft of educated leaders, were in the doldrums for the first half of the eighteenth century. Dr. Rufus Jones speaks of "the long quietistic period of the eighteenth century".[17] There was much confusion as to the right kind of organization for the sect, and attention was concentrated on discipline, minute matters of dress and behaviour being discussed at great length. On one matter, however, the Quakers began to give a lead and their sensitiveness to it was to be of untold benefit to England and to the whole Christian Church, which had all too long acquiesced in iniquity.

In 1671, George Fox had urged "Friends" in the West Indies to treat their slaves with humanity, and gradually the slave-trade and slavery itself became questions of special concern to the community. Most of their contemporaries—and even earnest Christians—long regarded this as a Quaker eccentricity. Slavery was accepted as an economic and political necessity. It was justified from the pages of the Old Testament. The Quakers, however, became more and more sure of the rightness of their repudiation of it. The saintly John Woolman began his protests in America as early as 1743.[18] In 1758 and again in 1761 London Quakers drew public attention to the iniquities of the system. In 1774, it

[17] *The Faith and Practice of the Quakers*, 1927, p. 56.
[18] He came to England in 1772 and died the same year in York. See A. M. Gummere, *Journal and Essays of John Woolman with biographical introduction*, 1922, and Janet Whitney, *John Woolman, Quaker*, 1943. His *Journal* and other writings are obtainable in the Everyman series.

was decided that any Friend who persisted in having deal-
ings with the trade should be expelled from the Society.
Two years later all Friends were ordered to set free their
slaves, a decision chiefly affecting those in America.

Already Granville Sharp was at work in England—a
dauntless champion of the negroes. By his persistence in
the case of the runaway slave, Somerset, he had so presented
the issue that Lord Chief Justice Mansfield had in 1772 (five
years after his judgment that Nonconformity was not a
crime) delivered judgment that "the state of slavery . . .
is so odious that nothing can be suffered to support it but
positive law " and that the law of England did not so support it, so that here the system could not be recognized and
all men were to be free. Two years later John Wesley spoke
out against the whole system—not only here, but anywhere.
In 1776, Adam Smith did the same. But these were individual voices. In 1781, the Quakers presented to Parliament
a petition against slavery, and two years later established
a standing committee of six to carry on continuous public
propaganda " for the relief and liberation of the Negro
slaves in the West Indies and for the discouragement of the
Slave Trade on the coast of Africa ". This committee
became the nucleus of the attack on the trade associated with
the names of Sharp, Clarkson and Wilberforce. All through
the long, fluctuating and difficult struggle, support for the
emancipators came in ever-increasing strength from the
Nonconformist communities. It is to the Quakers, however, that there belongs the honour of being always in the
van in a movement which, to use Trevelyan's words, " saved
civilization in three continents ".[19] Their efforts in this
cause lifted them to a position of leadership in social service
and in matters of conscience which has never been lost.

[19] Op. cit., p. 515. Cf. R. Coupland, The British Anti-Slavery
Movement, 1933.

CHAPTER SIX

Expansion: The Era of Napoleon and the Industrial Revolution

Some controversies which have long perplexed and divided the Church, are more clearly stated than ever; there are calls to preach the Gospel in many places where it has not been usually published; yea, a glorious door is opened, and is likely to be opened wider and wider, by the spread of civil and religious liberty, accompanied also by a diminution of the spirit of popery; a noble effort has been made to abolish the inhuman Slave Trade. . . . These are events that ought not to be overlooked; they are not to be reckoned small things.

WILLIAM CAREY,
Enquiry, 1792, pp. 79-80.

W E C O M E now to the era of Revolutions—the Industrial Revolution, the American Revolution, the French Revolution—one of the most significant periods in all human history and one which initiated rapid and fundamental changes in all departments of human life. It was in 1765 that James Watt first constructed the devices which revolutionized the steam-engine; within twenty years the first cotton factory was being run by steam and the era of modern industrialization had begun. People migrated from the country to the town, as the old village and home economy broke down. Population greatly increased. There was a rapid development of means of transport. Before anyone was aware of the social and economic changes that were in prospect, Britain lost her American colonies, and lost them largely through conservatism and short-sightedness. The great Declaration of Independence, drafted by Thomas Jefferson, was adopted in July, 1776, and seven years later Britain accepted the situation with as good a grace as possible.

" The American declaration of rights gave the cue to every friend of liberty in the old world," says H. A. L. Fisher.[1] Within six years of the ending of the American War the Paris mob stormed the gates of the Bastille, and overthrew the corrupt authority of the Bourbons and of the Roman Church in the name of Liberty, Equality and Fraternity. It was a time of excitement and expectation in Britain as well as in France, followed all too swiftly by the Revolutionary terror and then by the long, fluctuating struggle against Napoleon. When at last the Emperor was defeated at Waterloo in 1815, there came a period of reaction and bitterness. A social and economic revolution had been at work almost unperceived throughout the two decades of war. A heavy price had had to be paid for the defeat of Napoleon, and only gradually was it possible to press forward the struggle against civil and ecclesiastical privilege. Nonconformists, whose story is our special concern in these pages, moved in the early 1770's for relief from their continuing civil disabilities. They pressed with considerable expectation of success, but they failed, though supported by both the Earl of Chatham and Edmund Burke. It was not until 1828—two generations later—that at long last the Test and Corporation Acts were repealed. The following year Roman Catholics were accorded the right to sit in Parliament.

The half century from the war of American Independence

[1] *A History of Europe*, 1936, p. 791.

Student Christian Movement Press

56 Bloomsbury Street, London, W.C.1

THE EDITOR has much pleasure in sending a review copy of this book, the price of which is _____ 8/6 _____ net (in paper cover _____ net), and will be obliged if a copy of any notice that may appear is forwarded to him.

Where there are two editions it would be a favour if _both_ prices as given above could be quoted.

Publication Date _____ 2 JAN 1951 _____

to the repeal of the Test and Corporation Acts is a tumultuous period, crowded with exciting events and picturesque
personalities. Here it is possible to deal with only four main
matters that seem those of most significance for the development of the Free Churches, and their contribution to the life
of the modern world. First, we have to note the generally
sympathetic attitude of Nonconformists to the American and
French Revolutions, and their continued championship of
civil and religious liberty. Secondly, we shall see the
Evangelical Revival still at work and leading to a great
increase in the number of Nonconformists and to notable
evangelistic work in all parts of the country, not least in the
new industrial areas. Thirdly, there is to be noted—partly
as a result of the Revival, and partly as a result of the principles underlying the American and French Revolutions—a
new philanthropy, a new interest in education and social
reform, the beginnings of a concern for the victims of industrialization, in all of which Nonconformists took a prominent part. Finally, the period marks the beginning of the
modern expansion of the Christian Church overseas, and
here Baptists, Methodists and Congregationalists—in Britain
and in America—were in the van.

II

As we have already noted, the contacts between English
Dissenters and religious leaders in the American colonies
were close. Presbyterians, Independents, Baptists, Quakers,
were all numerous throughout the colonies. The Anglican
Church, which was the State-supported Church in the territories south of Delaware, excited growing antagonism for a
number of reasons, some of which might easily have been
remedied.[2] Nonconformists in England, with their own
grievances against the Established Church, were naturally

[2] See Nevins and Commager, *op. cit.*, pp. 64f.

predisposed to be sympathetic not only towards their co-religionists, but towards the colonists in general. But their sympathy and support were based on appreciation of the real issues involved and on a statesmanlike vision which was singularly lacking among the political and ecclesiastical authorities. Robert Hall had reason for the claim he made for Dissenters in 1793: "Had their remonstrance been regarded, the calamities of that (American) war had never been incurred."[3] Hall wrote with Dr. Richard Price particularly in mind, and he may well illustrate the attitude taken by the older Dissenting bodies and the importance of their service.

Price[4] was of Welsh origin but came to one of the London Dissenting Academies as a young man and remained in the metropolis all his life. He was never a great success as a pastor, partly because of the depression and ill-health from which he suffered; but his ability and sincerity gradually made him widely influential in the public life of the time. Priestley declared that Price had a celebrity "greater than any dissenting minister ever acquired before then". In 1757, when he was thirty-four, he wrote *A Review of the Principal Questions of Morals*, in which he urged that true virtue is possible only to those who are free. As his interests widened he had contacts with Lord Shelburne, David Hume and Benjamin Franklin and became a member of the Royal Society. Like Priestley he was a liberal in theology, but the two men were by no means always in agreement. Price took a deep interest in questions of finance and currency, and

[3] "Apology for the Freedom of the Press", *Works*, IV, p. 111.
[4] W. Morgan, *Memoirs of the Life of the Rev. Richard Price*, 1815, is stilted. A modern study by Roland Thomas appeared in 1924. Lincoln, *op. cit.*, Ch. IV, summarizes his political writings. For a modern estimate of his position as a moralist see W. H. F. Barnes, "Richard Price: A Neglected Eighteenth-Century Moralist", *Philosophy*, Vol. XVII, No. 66 (April, 1942). Price's *Review of the Principal Questions in Morals* was reissued by D. D. Raphael in 1948.

has been described as the founder of life insurance. His *Observations on Civil Liberty and the Justice and Policy of the War with America* (1776) is adjudged, apart from Tom Paine's *Common Sense*, " the most influential pamphlet of the American controversy ".[5] It brought him the freedom of the City of London and such popularity in America that he was invited by Congress in 1778 to go over there to organize the national finances. Four years later he is said to have been sought by the new premier, Lord Shelburne (Priestley's friend), as his private secretary and to have drafted at any rate one paragraph for the King's Speech. Pitt valued his judgment on financial matters.

Price's great fame came, however, in 1789 when he preached " On the Love of Our Country " at a service in commemoration of the English Revolution of 1688-9. It has been called " perhaps the most famous sermon of the century ",[6] for among its other consequences it provoked Burke's *Reflections on the French Revolution*. Price expressed the welcome to the French Revolution which was then general in large sections of the community, but apart from that the sermon is a courageous and lofty treatment of true patriotism. " Most of the evils which have taken place among bodies of men," he declared, " have been occasioned by their own interest overcoming the principle of universal benevolence." The sermon contains a denunciation of aggressive war, a plea for a representative federation of sovereign states, and a prophetic sketch of a confederation of the British Empire and a confederation of Europe. It

[5] Lincoln, *op. cit.*, p. 133.
[6] *Ibid.*, p. 129. Cf. H. N. Brailsford, *Shelley, Godwin and Their Circle*, 1913, p. 7: " The history of the French Revolution in England begins with a sermon." Brailsford, *ibid.*, p. 11, recalls that Condorcet regarded Price as one of the formative minds of the century. The text of the famous sermon is in: A. C. Ward, *A Miscellany of Tracts and Pamphlets*, World's Classics, 1927.

was not mere Utopianism, however. Price had a firm belief in a Heavenly City which is quite different from the most perfect on earth.[7] That he was—with many of his fellow countrymen, Wordsworth included—over-optimistic, that the French Revolution followed a sorry course, that many cherished liberties were endangered during the Napoleonic struggle, and that the gaining of others was long delayed, is no condemnation of the views expressed by Price in his famous discourse. The Revolutionary terror caused a swift revulsion of feeling and Nonconformists were soon once more the objects of popular abuse. Price was fortunate in that he died in 1791.

In the writings of Price, and those of his associates, the plea for liberty of conscience, first based on purely religious grounds, had gradually become a matter of natural right, something due to man as a child of God. Their general standpoint found expression in the American Declaration of Independence: " We hold these truths to be self-evident that all men are created equal, that they are endowed by their Creator with certain unalienable Rights, that among them are Life, Liberty and the pursuit of Happiness." In Britain this led Nonconformists to continue to demand full rights as citizens. When the 1772-3 demand, led by the Dissenting Deputies, failed, Nonconformists ceased to feel towards George III as they had felt towards his two predecessors. It was natural that they should support the growing demand for Parliamentary reform. But though charges of republicanism and later of Jacobinism were widely hurled at them, particularly by the Anglican clergy, they remained as loyal as ever, and it is significant that even in 1792 the gentle William Cowper wrote to Lady Hesketh: " Depend

[7] " All earthly governments have in them the seeds of decay and demolition." Cf. Niebuhr, *The Nature and Destiny of Man*, II, pp. 312f.

upon it, my dear, the hour is come when power founded in patronage and corrupt majorities must govern this land no longer. Concession too must be made to Dissenters of every denomination. They have a right to them, a right to all the privileges of Englishmen, and sooner or later, by fair means or by force, they will have them."[8]

During the Napoleonic wars Nonconformists successfully withstood attacks like that of Lord Sidmouth's bill against unlicensed preachers and did their best to preserve the dearly won liberties of their fellow subjects. In this connection two of Robert Hall's pamphlets are worth noting.[9] The writer was then in his early thirties. The first, published in 1791, is entitled *Christianity Consistent with a Love of Freedom*. It follows the general line of Price and Priestley. The second, *An Apology for the Freedom of the Press and for General Liberty*, was issued in 1793 as a reply to the Bishop of St. Asaph who had made a sweeping attack upon Dissenters. Hall reissued it in 1821, thus giving it a new lease of life when Nonconformists had begun their final campaign for civil and religious equality. So widespread did the demand then become that it was the Tory ministry of Wellington that had at length to repeal the Test and Corporation Acts and to grant Catholic Emancipation.

III

By the 1820's the number of Nonconformists had very greatly increased. Throughout the Napoleonic era the Methodist Revival continued on its course and in all denominations there were signs of vigorous, aggressive, expanding life. "The ultimate consequence (of the Methodist

---

[8] Letter from Weston Underwood, December 1st, 1792. Cf. Cowper's burning lines in *Expostulation*, 1782, against making attendance at Communion "an office-key, a pick-lock to a place".
[9] *Works*, Vol. IV.

Revival)," says Trevelyan, " was that the Nonconformists rose from about a twentieth of the church-goers to something near a half."[10]   And with this there has to be taken into account the rapid increase in the population. By 1815 there were nearly three times as many Methodists as at the time of Wesley's death, and they were represented in every part of the country.[11] His preachers had found their way into the growing towns in the Midlands and the North, and met the challenge of the redistribution of population with which the Established Church seemed powerless to cope. In many of the new factory and mining areas they had the field to themselves.[12]

Methodism, as we have seen, was originally conservative in its political outlook. It took its colour from the strongly expressed views of John Wesley, who supported the Crown against the American colonists, and who built up an organization essentially autocratic and centralized. As the movement spread, and particularly as it came to include large numbers of the working-classes, it proved more and more difficult to control on precisely the lines laid down by the founder. Dissentient groups hived off—the Methodist New Connexion in 1797, the Primitive Methodists in 1810, the Bible Christians in 1815—each of these movements largely inspired by more democratic ideas than the old guard of Methodism were ready to accept. The Methodist Conference had, under Wesley's direction, consisted only of preachers. The people themselves had little or no say in

[10] *British History in the Nineteenth Century*, 1922, p. 25.
[11] For analysis of figures see Maldwyn Edwards, *After Wesley*, 1935, Appendix I. Cf. Bebb, *Nonconformity and Social and Economic Life*, 1935.
[12] Cf. the remark made some generations later to Bishop Hensley Henson by a Durham miners' leader who was a staunch Methodist : " We were not dissenters; there was nothing for us to dissent from." On the somewhat analogous American situation see W. L. Sperry, *Religion in America*, p. 114.

church matters. This the New Connexion tried to rectify. The Primitive Methodists claimed the right to hold large camp meetings of a kind popular in America, but offensive to the ministers of Burslem and neighbourhood. The Bible Christians came into existence because an attempt was made to restrain William O'Bryan in his eager evangelism in Devon, an evangelism that would take no note of circuit boundaries.

These more free and democratic movements, and others like them, have been sneered at as evidence of "the dissidence of Dissent",[13] but they were a sign of the new religious life pulsing through the country-side. They came partly from increasing Methodist contact with the older Dissenters, partly from the ferment of revolutionary ideas then at work in the lower classes, partly from the almost despotic manner in which orthodox Methodism was governed. The outstanding figure in the second main period of its history was Jabez Bunting, and though his leadership continued until the middle of the nineteenth century and thus beyond our immediate period, he may here be mentioned. Bunting has been described as "the premier of Methodism who never went out of office, whoever might do so, having never been appointed". He had a profound distrust of the democratic movement in both Church and State, and is even said to have avowed in 1827 that "Methodism was as much opposed to democracy as it was to sin". Yet though views like this contributed to make Methodism the steadying anti-revolutionary force which, as

[13] The phrase was first used by Burke in his *Conciliation with America*, 1775, and was applied by him to the religious denominations in the American colonies. Hensley Henson, *The Church of England*, 1939, p. 3, speaks of our English racial individualism taking "the morbid form of fissiparous sectarianism". But see p. 178 below. On Methodist divisions and progress see Piette, *op. cit.*, pp. 393f.

H

Halévy points out, it undoubtedly was, there is clearly truth in Dr. Maldwyn Edwards's claim that, in spite of the dominant Toryism, there was an underlying liberalism in the movement. It was a movement which reached and evangelized the common people and gradually they found ways of making themselves vocal through it.[14]

As Methodists increased in numbers, so did Baptists and Congregationalists, and, for a time, those Presbyterian churches which joined the Unitarian Society. The strength of the last named was particularly noticeable in the north of England and among the new manufacturing classes.[15] Congregationalists, by the end of the eighteenth century, found most of their old meeting-houses full once more, and in all parts of the kingdom there was an era of chapel building. Not a few of the congregations gathered by Whitefield joined the ranks of the Congregationalists, as did later many of the churches of the Countess of Huntingdon's Connexion. In theology the rigid Calvinism of an older generation began to disappear. " The old Calvinistic phrases, the old Calvinistic definitions, were still on the lips of the Independents when George III died," says R. W. Dale; " but in the spirit and tendency of their theology they were Calvinists no longer."[16] Similarly there were subtle changes in polity. The classic Congregational emphasis on the privileges and responsibilities of the local church gave place to a much more casual individualism. Nevertheless, in the period under review the striking thing was growth and expansion.

Similar conditions prevailed among the Baptists. It was

[14] For the above paragraphs see Edwards, *op. cit.*, E. R. Taylor, *Methodism and Politics, 1791-1851,* 1935, and R. F. Wearmouth, *Methodism and the Working-Class Movements of England, 1800-1850,* 1937.
[15] See Raymond Holt, *op. cit.*
[16] *History of Congregationalism,* p. 588.

estimated that in the 1780's and early '90's J. C. Ryland and his son, John Ryland, ministers in Northampton, started regular services in no less than fifty Midland villages where, up till then, there had been no evangelical preaching, and before long most of the villages had chapels in them. In all parts of the country the same thing was happening. Baptists also gathered strength in the industrial districts. New associations were formed, and the earliest attempts at a national organization were made. Both Baptists and Congregationalists founded new colleges for the training of their ministers.

The Quakers had discovered a new sense of mission in their opposition to slavery and war, and their awakened social conscience. The quietness of their worship, and the simplicity of their dress and manners began again to make an appeal. In his respectful and sympathetic references to the Quakers, Charles Lamb spoke for many of his contemporaries.

In short, the Nonconformity that in 1828 secured the repeal of the Test and Corporation Acts was a much more numerous and vigorous body, representing a much larger section of the nation than that which had presented the same demand half a century earlier.

IV

Gradually the Revival deeply influenced a small but important section of the Anglican Church. During Wesley's life there were clergymen like Madan, Romaine, Grimshaw, Venn, Newton, Scott and Simeon, who, whilst full of sympathy for the new evangelical enthusiasm, were not prepared to break with the Establishment. In association with them there came into existence the famous " Clapham Sect ", a group chiefly of laymen, with Wilberforce at their centre, who gave themselves to philanthropy and humanitarianism, relying in the early stages of their many crusades very largely on Nonconformist support. There had been occasional intellectual contacts and collaboration between Anglicans and Dissenters in the quieter periods of the eighteenth century. This practical co-operation was new. It was significant of that breaking away from snobbery and tradition that characterized the Revival generally. But the change went deeper. A new division between the enemies and the professors of " vital godliness " cut across the older separation. In not a few towns evangelical Anglicans and Dissenters were ready to fraternize and even to worship together. Robert Hall, the noted Baptist preacher, may be taken as an example. It was estimated that his evening congregation in Leicester between the years 1808 and 1826 contained more than a hundred " pious members of the Church of England, and some of the neighbouring clergy frequently attended ". Hall himself, though he strongly dissented from an established Church, and was shocked by the corruptions of the Church of England, entirely rejecting " prelacy as it now subsists ", was yet ready to approve " occasional conformity " after the tradition of Baxter and Howe.[17]

Practical co-operation in the fight against the slave-trade and slavery has already been noted. The first phase of the struggle lasted from 1783 to 1807, when at last the labours of Wilberforce and his friends were crowned by an Act prohibiting the trade throughout the British Empire. " Without the aid of Nonconformist sympathy, and money, and oratory, and organization," said Sir George Trevelyan, " their operations would have been doomed to certain failure."[18] Throughout the country Nonconformists were

[17] *Works*, I, pp. 98 and 119. On the new alignment in general see C. Smyth, *Simeon and Church Order*, 1940.

[18] *Life and Letters of Lord Macaulay*, 1876, popular edition, 1893, p. 45.

ready to organize petitions, pass resolutions and create a public opinion demanding, in the face of opposition from many Anglican leaders, the ending of the trade; similarly, in the second phase of the struggle, that against slavery itself, which began in 1823. Again Nonconformist agitation—this time reinforced by intimate knowledge of what was going on in the West Indies—counted for a great deal in the final achievement of emancipation. Beside T. F. Buxton, who had succeeded Wilberforce as Parliamentary leader, John Smith of Demerara, and William Knibb of Jamaica, have an honourable place in the roll of the abolitionists.

But Nonconformists were growingly concerned not only for their own rights and for the rights of slaves many thousands of miles away. A social conscience was awakening as to conditions at home. It showed itself first in regard to children. Robert Raikes, a Gloucester printer and journalist, appalled at the ignorance and vice he saw among the local boys and girls, who were already at work from the tenderest years, had in 1780 gathered them together on a Sunday to teach them reading and writing and the rudiments of religion. Within a few years Sunday Schools sprang up all over the country, and whilst no one would wish to decry the work of Hannah More and other evangelical Anglicans, there is no doubt that it was among Nonconformists that they had their earliest and most striking successes, and that out of the Sunday School movement there developed a renewed interest in popular education which later was of great importance. The new movement gave a fillip to what had been attempted spasmodically, and often unsatisfactorily, by the charity schools of the eighteenth century. It was from the work of the British and Foreign School Society (1807, 1814), which relied largely on Quaker and Nonconformist support, and the National Society (1811), its Anglican rival, that there came, later in the nineteenth century, the demand for a truly national system of education.[19]

Closely akin to this interest in education was the movement for the provision of Bibles and of Christian literature. Both the Religious Tract Society (1799) and the British and Foreign Bible Society (1804) were interdenominational organizations in which evangelical Churchmen and Nonconformists served side by side. The same was true in the work for prison reform associated chiefly with the names of John Howard, a Dissenter, who " conformed " in 1773 that he might take office as High Sheriff of Bedfordshire and thus secure the right to visit prisoners, and Elizabeth Fry (née Gurney), the heroic Quakeress.

One of the most interesting evidences of an awakening social conscience is too often overlooked, namely, Nonconformist encouragement of the earliest efforts of sweated workpeople to obtain better conditions of livelihood. Two illustrations may be given. In the grim period between 1800 and 1825 it was regarded as illegal for workmen to associate together. Robert Hall, probably the most famous pulpit orator of his day, has already been referred to for his defence of the freedom of the press in 1793 and his contacts with evangelical Anglicans. In 1819, while minister in Leicester, he was so distressed at the pitiful condition of the local stocking makers that he issued an *Appeal to the Public on the subject of the Frame Work Knitters' Fund*. The low wages offered and the uncertainty of the work caused grievous distress. To meet periods of unemployment the workers had established a fund to which they contributed sixpence a week, and it was to augment this that Hall appealed, vigorously replying two years later to the objections raised by Cobbett and others, and asserting the right

[19] Cf. Halévy, Bk. III, Ch. II. and M. G. Jones, *The Charity School Movement*, 1938.

of the wage-earners to combine in self-defence.[20] The other illustration comes from Gloucestershire. In 1825-6 there were troubles around Nailsworth between manufacturers and weavers, and in the ensuing riots the soldiery were called out. Not a few of the workers were honoured members of the local Nonconformist Church, and when, three years later, a union was formed by the operatives in the district, though their meetings were held at the local ale-houses, " prayer was usually offered at the commencement and hymns sung ".[21] Trade-unionism was indeed, as we shall see further in the next chapter, cradled in Nonconformity. It was the distinction of Dissent that in the early years of the Industrial Revolution it gave to the new working class practical sympathy and support as well as the spiritual consolations of the gospel. Writing of the mass of unregarded humanity in the factories and mines of what he calls "Cobbett's England", Professor Trevelyan declares that "no one but the Nonconformist minister was their friend ".[22]

v

Probably, however, the most notable development of the period up to 1828 was the birth of the modern missionary movement, which was to carry the gospel to the remotest parts of the heathen world and lay the foundations of the modern world-wide Church. Protestantism had been singularly blind to the spiritual conditions of those in distant corners of the earth. In the eighteenth century the few who sought to preach to those of other races—the Pietists of Halle, the Moravians, the missionaries to the American Indians—were regarded by most of their fellow Christians

[20] *Works*, IV, pp. 167f. Cf. *Historical Illustrations of the Social Effects of Christianity*, Copec Report, Vol. XII, 1924, pp. 132f.
[21] F. T. Smythe, *Chronicles of Shortwood*, 1916, pp. 44f.
[22] *English Social History*, 1944, p. 476.

as queer misguided enthusiasts. The voyages of Captain Cook brought to Englishmen a new awareness of distant lands. Forces inherent in Calvinism at its best and in Methodism, with its leader claiming from the very beginning " the world as his parish ", prepared the way for the starting of missionary enterprises in the last decade of the eighteenth century.

The story is a remarkable one.[23] William Carey, a simple Baptist pastor of the Midlands—one who had been a shoe-maker and who still kept a school to supplement his small salary—had the honour of taking the lead in forming the first society to make the evangelization of the heathen world its aim. The Baptist Missionary Society was formed in October, 1792, a year after the Priestley riots, just as Britain was beginning her struggle with Revolutionary France. Carey himself went to India in 1793 and spent more than forty years there, leaving behind him a unique achievement as a translator, an evangelist, an educator, and a social reformer, maintaining to the last his simple but sturdy Non-conformity, in spite of the honours that came to him. After an unsuccessful mission to Sierra Leone, the B.M.S., in 1813, added Jamaica to its fields. In 1795, the London Missionary Society was founded—supported by Congregationalists, Scottish Presbyterians and a few evangelical Anglicans. Its efforts were directed to the South Seas and, a few years later, to South Africa and India. The notable Declaration adopted by the L.M.S. in 1796, and adhered to ever since, lays down its policy. " Our design is not to send Presby-terianism, Independency, Episcopacy, or any other form of

[23] For the whole section see E. A. Payne, *The Church Awakes*, 1942, and " The Evangelical Revival and the Modern Missionary Movement ", *Congregational Quarterly*, July, 1943. Cf. P. T. For-syth, *The Work of Christ*, second edition, p. 61, for comment on the fact that modern Protestant missions began with a group which was Calvinistic in theology.

Church Order and Government (about which there may be differences of opinion among serious Persons), but the Glorious Gospel of the Blessed God to the Heathen: and that it shall be left (as it ever ought to be left) to the minds of the Persons whom God may call into the fellowship of His Son from among them to assume for themselves such form of Church Government as to them shall appear most agreeable to the Word of God."[24] This meant a wide measure of ecclesiastical freedom in all the new Christian communities brought to birth through L.M.S. activity.

In 1799 the Church Missionary Society was formed on a specifically episcopal basis, and before long the older Anglican Society for the Propagation of the Gospel enlarged its scope, but it is fair to note that in the period under review it was the Nonconformists who rose most swiftly and enthusiastically to the challenge of overseas evangelism. Methodism had been interested in the work among the slaves ever since 1786, when the erratic Thomas Coke was driven by storms to Antigua. From then onwards Coke never rested in his efforts to promote missionary work till his sudden death in 1814 just as he hoped himself to begin work in India. By the time the Methodist Missionary Society was finally organized (1813-18), American Congregationalists were in the field, and soon afterwards American Baptists—the former in India, the latter in Burma. Societies were also formed on the Continent, and in 1824 the Foreign Missions Committee of the Church of Scotland started Presbyterianism on its work in India.

The period between the War of American Independence and the repeal of the Test and Corporation Acts was a truly revolutionary one in the life of man. In addition to great political and social changes, it saw a more vigorous and extensive demand for freedom of conscience than had ever

[24] Lovett, *History of the London Missionary Society*, I, p. 21.

before been made, a remarkable growth of the Free Churches here in England, and an awakening conscience regarding social ills. It saw also an extension of the Free Churches to Asia, Africa and the South Seas, from both England and America, that was fraught with the most important consequences for Christendom as a whole.

CHAPTER SEVEN

Confidence: The Victorian Age

I know the Dissenters. They carried the Reform Bill;
they carried the abolition of slavery; they carried Free
Trade; and they'll carry the abolition of Church Rates.

LORD JOHN RUSSELL,
Prime Minister 1846-52 and 1865-66.

In the long run English politics will follow the consciences of the Dissenters.

LORD PALMERSTON,
Prime Minister 1855-58 and 1859-65.

NONCONFORMISTS ARE seldom flattered on the few
occasions when they appear in Victorian literature.
Dickens, in the character of Stiggins, the odious " deputy
shepherd " in the *Pickwick Papers* (1837) and Chadband,
the eloquent but unpleasant humbug in *Bleak House* (1853),
satirized hypocrisy and priggishness, putting them in Nonconformist attire. Beside these portraits we may place his
description of a chapel: " It was not badly named in one
respect, being in truth a particularly little Bethel, a Bethel
of the smallest dimensions—with a small number of small
pews, and a small pulpit, in which a small gentleman (by
trade a shoemaker, and by calling a Divine) was delivering
in a by no means small voice, a by no means small sermon,
judging of its dimensions by the condition of his audience,
which if their gross amount were but small comprised a still
smaller number of hearers, as the majority were slumber-
ing." Charlotte Brontë imports humour into her descrip-

tion in *Shirley* (1849) of the meeting of rival Sunday School processions, but even she cannot avoid one or two ill-natured and unworthy sneers at the Dissenters. Charles Kingsley shows deep aversion, if not spite, in his account of the circle from which came the mother of the hero in *Alton Locke* (1850). In the melodramatic *Salem Chapel* (1863), Mrs. Oliphant, using her personal knowledge of a Church of Scotland congregation in Liverpool, gave a picture that has been widely accepted as a faithful delineation of the Congregationalism of the period; but in spite of the praise of so keen a critic as Robertson Nicoll, the young minister, Arthur Vincent, and even the deacon Tozer, must be regarded as caricatured rather than portrayed.[1]

Tennyson's " heated pulpiteer " in " Sea Dreams ", his preacher Muggins in " The Northern Cobbler ", and " the Baptises " in " The Church Warden and the Curate " can none of them be called complimentary allusions. Even Browning, though his own parents were Nonconformists, and though Elizabeth Barrett always spoke gratefully of Paddington chapel, which she and her sisters regularly attended, cannot be said to give an attractive picture of the worshippers in Zion chapel on Christmas Eve, 1849. Matthew Arnold's pages afford plentiful illustrations of condescending and even contemptuous polemic against English Nonconformity and Puritanism.[2] It is true that Carlyle must not be forgotten. " His presentation of Puritanism and the commonwealth and Oliver Cromwell ", in the words of John Morley, " first made the most elevating period of the national history in any way really intelligible."[3] But

[1] See Everyman edition with introduction by Robertson Nicoll. On the connections between the Brontë family and Methodism, see G. E. Harrison, *The Clue to the Brontës*, 1948.

[2] For a reply written in 1870 see R. W. Dale, " Mr. Matthew Arnold and the Nonconformists ", *Essays and Addresses*.

[3] *Miscellanies*, I, p. 140.

Carlyle was not writing of Cromwell's nineteenth-century descendants.

Elizabeth Gaskell and George Eliot stand almost alone among the writers of the period in treating contemporary Nonconformity with respect and sympathy. Both spoke of what they knew. Mrs. Gaskell was the daughter of a Unitarian manse and married a Unitarian minister. Her stories, which appeared between 1848 and 1865, gave a sympathetic account of the industrial life of the north of England. As a girl in Coventry, George Eliot attended a school kept by the daughters of a Baptist minister, Francis Franklin. Her own aunt was the original of the fine character, Dinah Morris, the deeply religious Methodist woman-preacher, in *Adam Bede* (1859). In *Silas Marner* (1861), in spite of the narrowness and harsh blindness of the Lantern Yard community, there is real recognition of its strength and sincerity. In *Felix Holt* (1866), she draws the full-length portrait of a Dissenting minister, Rufus Lyon, modelling him upon Francis Franklin, and it is a singularly attractive figure that emerges.

From a few years later come the not unsympathetic references to Nonconformists in the pages of Thomas Hardy. Clearly he recognized the strength and sincerity of those who had given many martyrs to Wessex and who took their religion with great seriousness. " Chapel-folk be more hand-in-glove with them above than we," says one of the characters in *Far from the Madding Crowd* (1874). To which his companion answers: " Yes, we know very well that if anybody do go to heaven, they will. They've worked hard for it, and they deserve to have it, such as 'tis. I bain't such a fool as to pretend that we who stick to the Church have the same chance as they, because we know we have not." Side by side with this passage may be set the rather grim description of believer's baptism in *The Laodicean* (1881) and the generous picture of Mr. Woodwell, the minister, which Mrs. Hardy says is "among the few portraits of actual persons in Hardy's novels". The references in George Eliot and Thomas Hardy cannot, however, be regarded as adequate compensation for the sins both of omission and commission in the pages of other writers. When every allowance has been made, it is clearly a very distorted picture of the religious and social life of the period which is to be found in its literature.[4]

The Victorian age saw a deepening of the cleavage between Nonconformists and Anglicans, and their mutual antipathy, the causes of which will shortly occupy us, was associated with much that was petty and discreditable on both sides. Yet those who were fighting for recognition and equality, those who were so frequently despised and ridiculed, and often shamefully victimized, probably gained much in moral stamina from their experiences. Professor Brogan's words are worth noting in this connection: "When the economic and other power that the squire and the parson then had is reflected on, there is something heroic in the ugly, poor and now neglected chapels that can be seen in so many English villages in East Anglia, Somerset and other strongholds of Puritanism. . . . Religious Dissent, accompanied by hardships that are serious but not demoralizing, is good education in real radicalism. . . . To be a minority, if not of active and convinced Christians, at least of the run-of-the-mill conforming Christians, to belong to bodies that were in varying degrees unfashionable in a country where snobbery is the rival religion to Christianity, to be forced to accept companions, to go to schools, to conform to social customs below the social level which your

[4] From the last decade of the nineteenth century come the novels of Mark Rutherford—*The Revolution in Tanner's Lane* (1887), *Miriam's Schooling* (1890) and *Catherine Furze* (1893)—with their picture of Nonconformist life half a century earlier.

financial status and education made natural to you: this was to receive a character building education not provided in many public schools. Nonconformity is in this context a more important phenomenon than mere Dissent."[5] This indicates one of Nonconformity's greatest services to nineteenth-century England, but it was a service which cost a great deal. There is truth in the remark of Augustine Birrell, whose father was a much respected Baptist minister in Liverpool in the middle decades of the nineteenth century, that it required a great effort to be a Nonconformist since it involved cutting oneself off " not from the fountains of holiness, but from the main currents of secular life ".[6]

II

The Test and Corporation Acts had been on the statute-book for a century and a half. Their repeal in 1828 marked the end of a long and often renewed struggle, but it did not give Dissenters full religious equality. There remained a number of important specific grievances as well as a continuing and embittering sense of social inferiority. Rates could be levied in any parish by a majority of the parishioners for the upkeep of the fabric of the Established Church. Marriages could be celebrated only by Church of England clergymen. Burials in churchyards could only be according to the Prayer Book service. Most charitable and educational endowments were in the hands of the Establishment. Oxford and Cambridge Universities remained closed to any but professed Anglicans. If all these matters, and particularly the last, could have been dealt with immediately after the repeal of the Test and Corporation Acts, the religious history of Victorian England would have been very

[5] *The English People*, pp. 126-7.
[6] Quoted by L. E. Elliott Binns, *Religion in the Victorian Age*, 1936, p. 73. Cf. Birrell, *Things Past Redress*, 1937.

different. But the ecclesiastical authorities were hostile to any and every concession. They were genuinely alarmed at the growth of Nonconformity. And Nonconformity—the new Nonconformity of the towns—was strong and aggressive and came increasingly to look upon the Establishment as a thoroughly evil institution, the enemy of all progress, political as well as religious. Relations between Nonconformists and Anglicans became worse, not better, in the decades following 1828.

Disputes over the possession of an endowed chapel in Wolverhampton, which began in 1816, had broadened into a spate of litigation, which finally led, in 1844, to the passing of the Dissenters' Chapels Bill, confirming in possession of buildings and endowments those who had made use of them for twenty-five years. Those who benefited more immediately from the measure were the Unitarians, but it gave to all churches freedom from the stranglehold of ancient trust deeds and from the fear of hostile legal proceedings.

Slowly but surely Nonconformity won its way forward and the established Church had to surrender first one and then another of its ancient privileges. Church Rates were abolished in 1868. Oxford and Cambridge were opened to Nonconformists and Roman Catholics in 1871. Nine years later, in 1880, the Burials Act removed the last of the minor grievances. But all these changes had to be fought for and were strenuously resisted. Inevitably the controversies left an unhappy legacy of bitterness on both sides. At the beginning of Victoria's long reign, Nonconformists were full of confidence that the Church would soon be disestablished. Joseph Angus, an able and outstanding nineteenth-century Free Churchman, began his public career by a prize essay on "The Voluntary System" (1839), which prophesied that twenty years was "the utmost limit" before the public establishment and endowment of religion would be ended and Church and State be completely separated. "Come it must," he declared, "and upon the zeal and enlightened devotedness of Christians it depends whether it be speedily in peace, or later in tears and in blood."[7] The disruption which occurred in the Church of Scotland in 1843, when, under the leadership of Thomas Chalmers, four hundred and seventy ministers left the security of the Presbyterian Establishment and formed a Free Church, seemed to confirm the view that the days remaining to the Anglican Establishment would be few.

In 1844, the British Anti-State Church Association was formed, which nine years later became the Liberation Society. It was under its auspices that most of the struggles for full civil and religious rights were conducted. Inevitably it had to initiate political and Parliamentary action. Edward Miall was a typical figure of this phase of Nonconformity's history. After some years in the Congregational ministry, he gave himself wholly to platform and journalistic work and was twice elected as a Liberal M.P., each time for a north of England industrial constituency. He lived long enough to see the passage of the Burials Act, long enough also to see that disestablishment would take far longer to secure in England than it had done in Ireland and that the " Oxford Movement " had brought a new spirit and temper —at once more intransigent and more genuinely religious— into the Church of England.

Their growing number, as well as the increasing demand for full equality of status, led, during the same period, to the closer organization of the different groups of Nonconformists. Representatives of Baptist churches had formed a union in 1813, but it had not had a very effective life. The organization was reconstituted in 1831, and in the same year

[7] *Op. cit.*, p. 207. On the controversies of this period see W. G. Addison, *Religious Equality in Modern England*, 1944, Ch. VI-XI.

the Congregational Union was formed. The general aims and methods of the two bodies were very similar. That of the Congregationalists had a sevenfold objective. First it sought " to promote Evangelical Religion, in connection with the Congregational Denomination ". Then, after various domestic objectives have been specified, the constitution states the last aim to be " to assist in maintaining and enlarging the civil rights of Protestant Dissenters ".[8] During most of the Victorian Era, in both the Baptist Union and the Congregational Union, the matter of civil rights naturally bulked large. It was not until the present century that other and more important lines of service began to open up for these Unions and that their implications for congregational theory began to be discussed. Methodists, during the middle decades of the nineteenth century, were much occupied with internal differences, many of them the product of the autocratic rule of Jabez Bunting. The last of the substantial secessions from the main stream of Methodism led, in 1857, to the establishment of the United Methodist Free Churches. But these dissensions, whilst they weakened, did not destroy Methodist evangelistic zeal.

Side by side with the Congregationalists, the Baptists and the various Methodist bodies, several new groups had appeared. There were, for example, the followers of Edward Irving, a young Scotsman whose preaching took London by storm in the 1820's.[9] Irving came to believe in the millennial interpretation of the books of Daniel and Revelation, and in the continuance of gifts of tongues, healings, and prophecy. Repudiated by the Presbyterian authorities, Irving and his friends organized the Catholic Apostolic Church which, though not large in numbers,

[8] Albert Peel, *These Hundred Years: A History of the Congregational Union of England and Wales*, 1931, pp. 63-4.
[9] See A. L. Drummond, *Edward Irving and His Circle*, 1937.

attracted for a time many wealthy and influential adherents. In 1844, seventy Presbyterian congregations—thirty-two in Northumberland and twelve in London—which had long looked towards Scotland for their religious affiliations, formed themselves into the Presbyterian Church of England and set about establishing with considerable success a home mission, a college and a foreign mission.[10] At about the same time the Plymouth Brethren came into existence, an anti-clerical and theologically narrow body aiming at recovering the simplicity and fervour of the early Church. Another contemporary movement, again an offshoot of Presbyterianism, was that of the Disciples or Churches of Christ, which was destined to become very strong in America. These movements and others that might be named, may be taken as evidence of the life that was in the Free Churches during the Victorian epoch, a life difficult to confine within traditional channels.

III

That Nonconformity had the ear of the ordinary man may be seen from the remarkable series of great preachers who came from its ranks in the second half of the century. They were the successors of men like Rowland Hill and Robert Hall, the outstanding preachers of the Napoleonic era. We may recall first one who was at the same time a great preacher, a theologian and a public figure, R. W. Dale, of Birmingham, who is described by H. W. Clark as " the finest and most spiritual nineteenth-century representative of the Nonconformist ideal ".[11] Dale combined moral fervour, intellectual power and intense religious conviction.

[10] S. W. Carruthers, *1844: A Tale of Faith and Courage*, 1944.

[11] *Op. cit.*, II, p. 415. See A. W. W. Dale, *Life of R. W. Dale*, 1899, aptly described by the late Professor J. Vernon Bartlet as " an integral part of the liberal education of any Congregationalist—indeed of all serious students of English religion and life ".

The whole of his ministerial life was spent in Birmingham and he came to have a unique influence not only within Congregationalism, but in local and national politics, as the ally and friend of the leaders of the Liberal Party, the vigorous embodiment of Nonconformity's interest in social and educational reforms. With the position Dale had in the Midlands we may compare that of Alexander McLaren, the Baptist, in Manchester, though his special fame rested not on his interest in public affairs but on his expository preaching. C. M. Birrell, of Liverpool, the father of Augustine Birrell, has already been mentioned. A more famous Liverpool figure was the Unitarian, James Martineau, who after twenty-two years there moved to London. Martineau[12] was a religious thinker of unusual power and insight and exercised a wide influence on the life of his time. He came to London in 1857, three years after young Spurgeon had arrived there.

Charles Haddon Spurgeon[13] was a unique figure in an age of great preachers. He was only twenty when he settled in London, but almost at once he became so popular that even the Exeter Hall could not hold his hearers. In 1861, the Metropolitan Tabernacle was built with accommodation for six thousand persons, and there Spurgeon ministered till his death in 1892. He was a Calvinist of evangelical views, free from the rigidity of the eighteenth-century Calvinist theologians, yet suspicious of Biblical criticism. Often he caused offence by his attacks on infant baptism and on some of his fellow Baptists, but his native gifts of pungency and humour, his matchless voice, and his unwearying evangelistic zeal, gave him an influence that has continued long after the personalities of most of his contemporaries have become dim.

[12] J. Estlin Carpenter, *James Martineau*, 1905.
[13] W. Y. Fullerton, *C. H. Spurgeon: A Biography*, 1920.

In the last decades of Spurgeon's life two other Nonconformist preachers made their mark in London, Joseph
Parker and Hugh Price Hughes. Parker was a Congregationalist with great dramatic power in the pulpit, somewhat
eccentric in manner and conservative in outlook, but with
a prophetic quality in his preaching that gave him a wide
influence. Hugh Price Hughes was a Methodist, the flaming apostle of Radicalism and "social Christianity", who
made plain how much Methodism had changed since the
days of Jabez Bunting. His work, more than that of any
of those already mentioned save perhaps Dale, links the
Victorian age with that of the opening years of the twentieth
century.

Dale, McLaren, Martineau, Spurgeon, Parker, Hugh
Price Hughes—they form a remarkable group, and their
influence on the religious outlook of the ordinary man in
nineteenth-century England, and throughout the English-
speaking world, it is impossible to over-estimate. Moreover,
in almost every large city there were Nonconformist
preachers who came to be regarded as in some measure the
guardians of the public conscience. Trevelyan does them
far less than justice when he speaks of them as " able men
embittered by a sense of ill-usage and ostracism ".[14] As
Professor Brogan points out: " No one else has succeeded
in doing what Nonconformity did, in giving a prosperous
bourgeoisie a sense of duty and a sense of social obligation."[15] This was the work of the Free Church preachers
of the nineteenth century. They contributed one of the
main influences to the making of the typical Victorian
middle-class citizen. To borrow the words of Troeltsch,
they showed how " to neutralize the ethically dangerous

[14] *British History in the Nineteenth Century*, p. 284.
[15] *The English People*, p. 130. Cf. E. H. Carr, *Conditions of Peace*,
1942, pp. 33, 121, etc., on the need of the twentieth century in this
connection.

consequences of modern life by the religious ideas of the responsibility of the individual, and of the duty of love, both of the individual and of the community, through the taboo on luxury, mammon, and love of pleasure, and finally through heroism in serving the cause of Christ all over the world ".[16]

That the message of these men had serious limitations and that they did not succeed in making England effectively Christian is of course true. Properly to assess their achievement we have to compare it with what the Anglican Church did during the same period. We have to remember that they were inevitably involved in the continued struggle for the removal of Nonconformist grievances and disabilities. We have, further, to bear in mind the tremendous intellectual as well as other changes that were taking place during the Victorian era.

IV

In 1828, the year of the repeal of the Test and Corporation Acts, John Henry Newman, then in his late twenties, became vicar of St. Mary's, Oxford. In the same year he first met John Keble, who in 1831 was appointed professor of Poetry in the University. Two years later, the first of the famous " Tracts for the Times " was issued and the " Oxford Movement " started on its course. The dates are significant in relation to the period under review, for it was the Oxford Movement with its renewed stress on Catholicism and tradition, its emphasis on the doctrine of the Church, and the spiritual devotion which it inspired, that gave new life to the Church of England. In the previous decades, it had been among the Evangelicals, the minority influenced by the Revival of the eighteenth century, that religious zeal and power were to be found. The Evan-

[16] *Social Teaching*, pp. 1011-12.

gelicals, as we have seen, were quite ready to fraternize and co-operate with Nonconformists, but by the 1830's they had lost their outstanding leaders and their message was becoming stereotyped. Apart from the Evangelicals, the National Church seemed to many lifeless, an effete institution, the supporter of privilege and reaction. Professor Brogan quotes the witticism that " the troubles of the Church of England in modern times are due to the fact that in its old age it has got religion ".[17] So far as this is true, it must be set down mainly to the influences flowing from the Oxford Movement, either directly or by reaction, though an independent factor was the tradition of " Christian Socialism " which began in the 1850's and was associated with F. D. Maurice, Kingsley and Ludlow.[18]

Nonconformists were naturally critical of the Oxford Movement which, in its early stages, fiercely attacked evangelicalism and seemed chiefly interested in the resuscitation of ancient forms, ceremonies and, as Nonconformists believed, superstitions. Newman and his friends challenged the Reformation itself, but it is significant that in the 1880's a Nonconformist leader of the intellectual and spiritual calibre of Dale was ready to say to his friend, Dr. Fairbairn: " The blessing of God was in it, though we did not see it, and in a form they did not understand; in the lives and in the devotion of these men a new endowment of the Holy Spirit came into the life of England."[19]

The Oxford Movement entirely changed the ecclesiastical situation in England. But there were other more profound changes at work, affecting all branches of the Church alike. The very foundations of the Christian faith seemed to be shaken by the discoveries and methods of the new sciences,

[17] The English People, p. 102.
[18] C. E. Raven, Christian Socialism, 1920.
[19] A. W. W. Dale, Life of R. W. Dale, 1899, p. 699.

those of geology, zoology and biology in particular. It was not until 1859 that Darwin published his epoch-making book, *The Origin of Species*. Excited public controversies followed, in which Huxley was the protagonist of science against bishops and other ecclesiastical leaders. But in the early decades of the nineteenth century the leaven of the new knowledge had been powerfully at work. The new discoveries and the theories based upon them challenged the scheme of Biblical chronology worked out by Archbishop Ussher in the seventeenth century and accepted by Christians generally. More important still, they seemed to invalidate the account of creation given in Genesis. We have already noted how much the old Dissenting academies had contributed to the interest in the natural sciences. The spirit of free inquiry fostered by Priestley and others made certain Dissenters at any rate ready to interest themselves in the new views, though inevitably there was heart-burning and mental bewilderment in many quarters. John Pye Smith, who taught at the Homerton Academy from 1806 to 1851, is worthy of note as one of the first to show a willingness to accept science as a revelation from God. Philip Gosse may be taken as an example of one who made important contributions to Natural History, but did so while retaining unaltered his beliefs as a Plymouth Brother.[20]

It was inevitable that once methods of scientific study had been developed they should be applied to the Bible itself as well as to the formularies of the Church. Biblical criticism —examination of the language and contents of the various books in relation to their contemporary setting, and study of the way in which the collection has been handed down from generation to generation—had begun in the eighteenth

[20] Gosse's dates were 1810-88. His son Edmund was born in 1849. The story of their relationship—a vivid and poignant revelation of the religious difficulties of the time—will be found in *Father and Son*, 1907.

century, and quickly developed in the early decades of the nineteenth. It raised searching questions for all Christians and cut across the ordinary ecclesiastical divisions. The Unitarians were, perhaps, the only body who, as such, were not involved in tribulation. All the others—the Church of England as well as the main Nonconformist bodies—found it far from easy to adjust themselves to a critical study of Scripture hitherto generally regarded as an unbroken unity and verbally infallible. The working out of a new theory of inspiration took a long time and has not really yet been completed. No branch of the Church totally rejected the new approach, though some of the smaller offshoots of the Free Churches remained extremely critical and conservative in regard to it. The kind of personal difficulties involved may be illustrated from the pages of Mark Rutherford, whose *Autobiography*, though written in 1881, reflects conditions thirty years earlier, or from the case of Samuel Davidson who was compelled to resign his position at the Lancashire Independent College in 1857 because of his liberal views, the case antedating by a quarter of a century the more famous one of Robertson Smith in Scotland.[21]

There were other minor theological controversies within Nonconformity such as that regarding conditional immortality with which the names of John Foster, the famous Baptist essayist, and Edward White, a Congregational minister, are specially connected; or that over the hymns of T. T. Lynch in the 1850's;[22] or the " Downgrade " controversy among the Baptists with which Spurgeon was connected in the '80's. All these controversies led in the end

[21] P. Carnegie Simpson, *The Life of Principal Rainy*, 1900, remains the most illuminating and authoritative account of the Robertson Smith case and of the religious history of Scotland during the nineteenth century.

[22] The so-called " Rivulet " controversy, from the sub-title of Lynch's *Hymns for Heart and Voice*, 1855.

to increased spiritual liberty, but they also contributed to the spread of agnosticism and secularism and to a somewhat wistful sadness which hangs over much Victorian thought. The years of discovery and controversy proved spiritually very exhausting. It is against this background that the achievement of the great Nonconformist preachers has to be studied.

V

The Nonconformity of the Victorian age, however, was significant not only for the successful struggle for full religious equality, and for a great preaching tradition maintained in an age of intellectual ferment and change, but also for its ethical emphasis and its practical service to the community.

Nonconformists continued to take a deep interest in education and were in the forefront of the movement for a national system under public control, in the provision of which England lagged sadly behind other nations largely because of the opposition of the National Church. In the first half of the century many new theological colleges were established which continued on broader lines the traditions of the eighteenth-century academies.[23] Nonconformists had a notable share in the establishment of University College, Gower Street, and in the development of London University. Later they were able to play a generous part in the movement which led to the provincial universities. As we have seen, Oxford and Cambridge at last opened their doors to them in 1871. The previous year an Education Act was passed by Gladstone's first Government, setting up a national system, but of a kind which gravely affronted Nonconformists and has been the cause of continued strife ever

[23] See E. A. Payne, "Nonconformist Theological Education in the Nineteenth Century" in *Studies in History and Religion*, 1942.

since. The scheme was the work of W. E. Forster. It made the existing voluntary schools, almost all of them the property of the Church of England, an integral part of the national system, doubled the existing grants to them, and put publicly controlled schools only in the places then unprovided for. The famous "Cowper-Temple" clause was a concession to Nonconformists, won in committee, and prohibited denominational teaching in provided schools. "There could be no reasonable doubt," says Dr. Hensley Henson, "as to the justice of this interpretation of the national mind."[24]

Linked with this interest in education may be set Nonconformity's concern for the welfare of children as seen not only in the development of Sunday Schools and youth organizations, but also in the provision of orphanages, of which in the Victorian era there were all too few. Outstanding were those associated with the names of George Müller, the Plymouth Brother, Spurgeon, the Baptist, T. B. Stephenson, the Methodist, and Dr. Barnardo,[25] whose chief religious connections were with the Brethren and the Baptists.

The temperance movement was a product of Victorian Nonconformity and one of which, considering the magnitude of the evils attacked, it has every reason to be proud. Here Methodists were in the van. John Wesley—in this respect far ahead of his time—had condemned spirit-drinking and had pleaded for the abolition of distilling. Most of his successors showed for some time little interest in this aspect of his teaching, but in 1830 Joseph Livesey and a group of friends—"the Seven men of Preston"—most of them Methodist lay preachers—took a pledge of total

[24] *The Church of England*, 1939, p. 197.
[25] See biographies by J. Wesley Bready, 1930, and A. E. Williams, 1943.

abstinence and set out to try to rescue the intemperate and to check some of the evils of indulgence. The frequent drinking of alcoholic beverages on a considerable scale was a generally accepted custom, and in its early years the temperance movement was violently attacked even in religious circles. The scornful references in the pages of Dickens may be better appreciated when it is recalled that in 1840 the Methodist Conference ordered two candidates for the ministry to forswear their teetotal convictions or else to withdraw.[26] Gradually, however, the movement grew in strength. Bands of Hope for children and adult temperance societies were started, and by the end of the century total abstinence was the general rule throughout the Free Churches, though there was considerable divergence of opinion as to the right way of tackling the social evils springing from the drink traffic.

In the early decades of the Victorian era, Nonconformity was far more closely in touch with the industrial population than was the Church of England. It was natural that Nonconformists, at any rate as individuals, should be connected with the beginnings of working-class agitation for the improvement of conditions of labour. The stand taken by Robert Hall a generation earlier has been already mentioned. Trade Unions did not become legal till 1824-5. Ten years later a group of labourers in Dorset who attempted to combine were savagely sentenced to transportation. Of the six "Tolpuddle Martyrs", as they came to be called, five were Methodists—three of them local preachers and one the owner of the local Methodist chapel.[27] The same period saw the prophetic movement known as Chartism, the main aims of which were annual parliaments and universal suffrage. The

[26] Maldwyn Edwards, *Methodism and England*, 1943, p. 105.
[27] For details see R. F. Wearmouth, *Methodism and the Working Class Movements of England*, 1937, pp. 265f.

working classes had discovered that the Reform Bill of 1832 left them still among the disfranchised and that little was to be done to remedy their condition. There were some ugly outbursts of violence, but in the end the movement collapsed. Dr. Maldwyn Edwards ascribes the failure largely to the refusal of so many workers to join the movement, and this in turn he ascribes to the fact that official Methodism reacted strongly against it and that Methodists were numerous in the Chartist areas. R. F. Wearmouth argues that it was its aloofness from radicalism that saved Methodism during these troubled years.[28] On the other hand, it is worthy of note that William Lovett and Thomas Cooper, two of the Chartist leaders, owed much to Methodism, and that one of their strongest supporters, and one who advocated the use of force, Joseph Rayner Stephens, was a Methodist minister. Much of the Chartist organization, and many of its methods, were borrowed from the religious societies and there was real religious feeling behind it.

Chartism was a working-class movement. In the same years Cobden and Bright were agitating for the repeal of the Corn Laws in view of the widely prevalent distress. They drew their support mainly from the middle classes, and in 1841 were able to assemble seven hundred Nonconformist ministers under the auspices of their Anti-Corn Law League. There were also close links between the store and the chapel in the early history of the Co-operative Movement, which began in Rochdale in 1844, though most of the pioneers were Unitarians or of somewhat unorthodox religious views.[29]

The development of Trade Unionism which followed the Chartist collapse, though slow, owed not a little to

[28] *Methodism and England*, pp. 43f. Wearmouth, *op. cit.*, pp. 129f.

[29] See G. D. H. Cole, *A Century of Co-operation*, 1944.

Nonconformity. It was men trained in self-discipline, self-government and self-expression in the chapels of the industrial areas who became the organizers and leaders. Sidney Webb is outspoken in his tribute to the part played by the Primitive Methodists first in Christianizing and civilizing the mining areas of Northumberland and Durham, and then in leading the miners in their fight for better conditions.[30] The miners' leader, Thomas Burt, who was elected Liberal M.P. for Morpeth in 1874 and who lived to become the "Father" of the House of Commons, was a staunch Primitive Methodist and an ardent teetotaller. William Abraham (Mabon), who reached Parliament in 1885 after being in the pits from the age of nine, was a recognized leader of Welsh Nonconformity. Joseph Arch, who "by his perseverance and energy did more than any other man of his time to improve the conditions of the agricultural workers",[31] and who established the Agricultural Workers' Union in 1872, was a Methodist local preacher. And these are but a few of the names which might be cited. In the great London dock strike of 1889, a young Baptist minister, J. C. Carlile, was able to join with Cardinal Manning in exercising a restraining influence on the men and helping to secure for them better conditions.

Just as the working-class movement sought the aid—often somewhat grudgingly given—of the Liberal Party, so did Nonconformity, for the securing of its own rights and for the furtherance of the interests it had at heart. In John Bright, the Quaker, it had its own representative in the highest councils of the party and in the Government itself. Bright, a man of outstanding Christian character, was the

[30] *The Story of the Durham Miners*, 1921.

[31] *Dictionary of National Biography*. Michael House, *In This Valley*, 1934, and *Autumn Fields*, 1944, gives a sympathetic picture of rural conditions in East Anglia in the closing decades of the nineteenth century, and the place there of the Nonconformist chapel.

first Nonconformist since William Penn to be prominent as a political leader. In the later decades of the century it was a Unitarian, Joseph Chamberlain, who emerged as the leader of Midland Radicalism. But though Nonconformity was closely linked with the Liberal Party and shared in the political perplexities over Home Rule for Ireland and other matters, it cannot truthfully be contended that it ever surrendered its independence. Nonconformity had a conscience of its own, functioning on a national scale through men like R. W. Dale and Hugh Price Hughes, and this conscience had already much to its credit long before the episode of the O'Shea divorce (1890), which drove Parnell from the leadership of the Irish Party and which brought the phrase "the Nonconformist conscience" into general use.[32]

He who would see the growing influence, the widening horizon and the increasing prosperity of Nonconformity during the Victorian period must turn to the Nonconformist press, and study in particular the *Nonconformist*, which Edward Miall founded in 1841 and which contained some of the early writings of Herbert Spencer, the *Christian World*, which began in 1857, Hugh Price Hughes's *Methodist Times,* started in 1885, and the *British Weekly*, which from 1886, though edited by a Scottish Presbyterian and influential north of the border, was published in England and rapidly secured wide support in all the Free Churches.[33] In this connection the influence exerted in the latter half of the century by the *Manchester Guardian* is important. Its great editor, C. P. Scott, came of an old

---

[32] See Maldwyn Edwards, *Methodism and England*, p. 185f., though he is exaggerating in saying that "it was Hughes who as much as any other man made the Free Churches a force in the national life", and H. Lovell Cocks, *The Nonconformist Conscience*, 1943.

[33] Cf. T. H. Darlow, *William Robertson Nicoll*, 1925, Ch. VI.

Unitarian family, his grandfather having been a close friend of Priestley, and this religious inheritance helped to give him his "power of putting all that concerned himself and his age *sub specie æternitatis*".[34]

VI

There is space for only a very brief final word on the continuing evangelistic impulse within Nonconformity. It showed itself in the preaching of Spurgeon and in the welcome given to Evangelists like D. L. Moody. It showed itself in the Salvation Army. It showed itself in the outstanding growth of the missionary movement during the nineteenth century.

Moody spent the two years from 1873-5 in this country conducting special missions with very notable success. In London, at the time, the Rev. William Booth, formerly an itinerant preacher of the Methodist New Connexion, was developing the work of a Christian Mission in the slums of Whitechapel. He and his wife felt the call to preach to the most neglected and degraded of the poor, and they were ready to use the most unconventional methods. They had recently been joined in their work by their eldest child, Bramwell, who had been born in 1856. It was in 1878 that their success in securing conversions led them to desire an organization that would enable them to work along their own authoritarian lines, and they adopted the name, " the Salvation Army ". They were soon launched on great campaigns in all the large cities, campaigns often attended with opposition and violence, partly because of the rough areas in which they were held, and partly because of the frank appeal to the emotions which was made. Throughout the remaining years of the century the Salvation Army

[34] See J. L. Hammond, *C. P. Scott of the Manchester Guardian*, 1934.

rapidly grew in strength, championing the cause of the increasing multitudes of the churchless in the slums, attacking vice and debauchery in any and every form and gradually breaking down the distrust with which it had at first been regarded. " General " Booth's book *In Darkest England* (1890) was a landmark in the expansion of the Army. It drew attention to the condition of the " submerged tenth ", the victims of an industrial prosperity built on the *laissez-faire* system, and successfully appealed for large sums of money in order to undertake rescue and ameliorative work.

The title of Booth's book was deliberately copied from *Darkest Africa* (1890), the account H. M. Stanley had just published of his great journey through Equatorial Africa to rescue Emin Pasha, who had been abandoned when the Mahdi overran the Sudan. Both books had an immense sale, the one focusing attention on the need for Christian evangelism in England and the other stimulating the missionary interest in Africa which had been rapidly growing during the century. " In geographic extent, in movements issuing from it, and in its effect upon the race," says Latourette, " in the nineteenth century Christianity had a far larger place in human history than at any previous time."[35] What at the beginning of the Victorian era was the concern of small groups of enthusiasts became a mighty stream of Christian enterprise flowing out by many channels to every part of the earth. In this remarkable expansion of the Christian religion, Free Churchmen had an honourable part. Names like those of Moffat, Livingstone, Saker and Comber, testify this in connection with Africa; Morrison, Legge, David Hill, Griffith John, Hudson Taylor, James Gilmour and Timothy Richard in connection with China; John Williams, J. G. Paton and James Chalmers in the South Seas. Congregationalists, Methodists, Baptists, and

[35] *History of the Expansion of Christianity*, V, p. 1.

Quakers—as well as representatives of smaller bodies—all had a share in the work. Through their labours there came into existence in Asia, Africa and elsewhere, Christian communities not only—as was naturally the case—free of any State connection, but non-episcopal in order and bound in no way to the see of Canterbury or the Anglican formularies, communities that could know little or nothing of the controversies which had so long divided Anglicans and Nonconformists in England. Moreover, to these communities must be added, for a true assessment of the growth of the Free Churches during the nineteenth century, the mighty increase in their numbers in the United States, the growth in the British colonies and dominions, and the results of the missionary work undertaken by the predominantly non-episcopal churches of America.

CHAPTER EIGHT

Hesitancy: 1900-1939

It is probable that Nonconformity reached its height of political power, was most representative of the temper of the English people, round the beginning of this century. . . . But in the generation that has passed since the great Liberal landslide of 1906, one of the greatest changes in the English religious and social landscape has been the decline of Nonconformity.

D. W. BROGAN,
The English People, p. 121.

To ATTEMPT to describe the happenings of the last forty or fifty years is both difficult and dangerous. One is too near the events properly to assess their importance, or to see them in perspective. Nevertheless, though a very different chapter on this period will no doubt be written at the end of the present century, it is important for our present purpose to chronicle certain developments and tendencies. The past four or five decades have been among the most dramatic and distressing of any in European history. The whole world has been involved in upheaval and strife. It may well be that future generations will recognize that once more an unstable age has been a great and creative age, but at the moment the shape of things to come remains too uncertain and we are too much involved in the crises of the moment to be sure of this. Men entered the twentieth century with enthusiasm and confidence, and Nonconformists in particular looked forward eagerly, for they had more liberty, prosperity and influence than ever before. The war of 1914-18 and that which began in 1939, and the forces of which these conflicts were but the expression, have shaken the very foundations of our civilization. They provide a vast, sombre and rather terrifying background against which to continue the story of the Free Churches.

Before they passed away, the great leaders of Victorian Nonconformity were responsible for two new developments which were prophetic of a new era. First, the various Free Churches formed world organizations to link them with their sister and daughter churches overseas, and, secondly, the Free Churches of Britain drew more closely together and established an organization for common council and action.

It was in 1877 that the General Presbyterian Alliance was founded to bring together in a federation all the Reformed Churches which are of the Presbyterian pattern. Four years later, the first Methodist Ecumenical Conference was held, and similar gatherings took place every ten years up to 1931. An International Congregational Council was assembled in 1891, with R. W. Dale as its Chairman, and this met again in 1899, 1908, 1920 and 1930. In 1905, with Dr. Clifford as Chairman and the aged Alexander McLaren as an honoured leader, Baptists formed the Baptist World Alliance, which, though the youngest, has been by no means the least vigorous of these organizations, and has brought together very large numbers of delegates in congresses in various cities in Europe and North America. All these bodies—as their names imply—are fraternal and consultative. They have little formal authority. Nevertheless, they effectively express the general consensus of opinion in the different communions. They were made possible by the increasing contacts between different parts of the world and the gradual emergence of a world-consciousness. They are the Free Church counterpart of the Lambeth Conferences of the bishops of the Anglican Communion which began in 1868, and their growth has been intertwined with that of the general " Ecumenical Movement ", which will concern us later.

The other development in Free Church life in the last decade of the nineteenth century—the establishment of the National Free Church Council and its local units—owed a great deal to Hugh Price Hughes to whom allusion has already been made, and to John Clifford, a noted Baptist leader. It began with a congress in Manchester in 1892, attended by some 370 Free Churchmen, more than half of whom were Congregationalists. Subsequent gatherings in Leeds (1894) and Birmingham (1895) led to the setting up of a loose network of councils all over the country. The annual assembly became " the free voice of Noncon-formity ",[1] but its membership was not made up on any representative principle so far as the different churches were concerned, nor was there any clear doctrinal or even practical basis. From the very beginning there were divergent forces at work within the movement, while the secular and reli-gious conflicts of the time drew to it the more militant wing of Nonconformity. "The Free Churches," said Silvester Horne, writing in 1903, " came together under the shadow of a great common peril "[2] and this he explains to be the Romanizing of the Anglican Church. Among the subjects which roused the greatest interest at early Congresses were attacks upon " sacerdotalism " and resolutions in favour of " disestablishment ". At the Leeds Congress in 1894 a speech on " The Labour Problem " caused considerable divergence of opinion.

Nonconformity was excited, confident, eager, as it entered

[1] Shakespeare, *The Churches at the Cross-roads*, 1918, p. 151. Cf. H. W. Clark, *op. cit.*, II, p. 424.
[2] *Popular History*, p. 424.

the twentieth century. Its social position had greatly improved. Its preachers were still eagerly listened to, though many of them had more to say of " the social gospel " than of evangelical experience, and more of Biblical criticism than of theology. Oxford and Cambridge Universities were now open to its sons, and in municipal and national politics there were opportunities for the able and ambitious of a kind unknown before. Money was more plentiful in Nonconformist pockets, and at the turn of the century, Methodists, Baptists and Congregationalists were all able to raise large central funds. " The whole Ecclesiastical History, from the first century of the Christian Church," said Defoe in 1701, " is full of instances to confirm this, That the Prosperity of the Church of Christ has been more fatal to it than all the Persecution of its Enemies."[3] But the signs of this, so far as twentieth-century Nonconformity was concerned, were as yet only on the horizon.

The prospect seemed fair. There had been some difference of view regarding the Boer War. Mr. Balfour's Education Act of 1902 gravely affronted Free Church sentiment by entrenching the Anglican-owned schools in the national system, and led to a Passive Resistance movement which took many Nonconformist ministers to prison or led to distraint upon their goods because of refusal to pay a proportion of their rates. But these things, it was believed, would soon be put right, and indeed the 1906 election swept the Liberal Party into power, and the new Parliament contained more Nonconformists than had been there since the days of Cromwell. The rising leaders of the party were of Nonconformist origin—Asquith, Simon, Runciman, Lloyd George, Hewart and others. A Nonconformist, Lord Cozens Hardy, whose daughter had married Silvester Horne, a Congregational minister, became Master of the

[3] *Discourse on Occasional Conformity,* pp. 8-9.

Rolls. Political Nonconformity hoped that before long its education grievances would be redressed and meantime bent its energies to the securing of the disestablishment of the Church of Wales, as a step towards a similar measure in England. The Welsh Church Bill was bitterly opposed. Yet seeing that the overwhelming majority of Welshmen were Nonconformist in sentiment, it cannot rightly be described as unjust or ungenerous. The effects of disestablishment have not been according to the expectations of either friends or foes. Since 1920 there have been many signs of new spiritual vigour in " the Church in Wales ", which now has an Archbishop of its own, whereas Nonconformity has not its former power. How far this is due to the general conditions of the time and how far to more specifically ecclesiastical issues it is too early to say.

When the Conservative Party took advantage of its influence in the House of Lords to hold up the financial and social legislation of the Liberal Government, the curtailment of the privileges of the Upper House became an issue, and Nonconformists were as ready to join in the struggle on the one side as were most Anglicans on the other. A curious illustration of the temper of the time may be found in the preface to Silvester Horne's *Popular History of the Free Churches* (1903), which invites Nonconformists to imitate the valour of their seventeenth-century forbears in an attack upon " an hereditary House of Peers, in which no single Free Churchman has a place, and which is an effective instrument against popular privilege and progress ".[4] Religious and political excitement rose throughout the opening decade of the twentieth century, and the nation became deeply divided, not only over the position of the Lords, but also over Irish Home Rule, which had complicated and embittered English political life for more than a generation.

[4] *Op. cit.,* p. viii.

It was upon an England in the throes of a grave constitutional crisis, with the Church of England still ranged in the main solidly behind the Conservative Party and the Nonconformists enthusiastically assisting the Liberals, that there suddenly burst, with such warnings as there had been almost completely unheeded, the war of 1914-18.

II

The typical Free Church figures of the earlier part of the period were John Clifford and Silvester Horne.[5]   The latter was a gifted and radiant personality, one of the earliest students at Mansfield College, Oxford, who as soon as his course was over settled at one of the leading Congregational churches in London.   During the struggle over the Education Bill of 1902, his brilliance as a platform orator gave him a national reputation, and in 1910 he entered the House of Commons, whilst still retaining his superintendence of Whitefield's Tabernacle.   His prodigal spending of his strength had inevitably to be paid for.   In the spring of 1914, while on a trip to Canada, he suddenly dropped dead, though only forty-nine years old, leaving a strangely personal sense of loss in the hearts of thousands.

 Of Clifford more should be said.   " His was the voice," says a shrewd and sympathetic observer, " of fighting Non-

---

[5] See W. B. Selbie, *C. Silvester Horne*, 1920, and Sir James Marchant, *Dr. John Clifford, C.H.*, 1924.   Both Horne and Clifford appear in E. H. Jeffs, *Princes of the Modern Pulpit*, 1930, together with a number of other Nonconformists influential during the first thirty years of the century.   The novelists of the period have been little more kind or understanding than their Victorian predecessors. References to the Nonconformity of the Midlands and North of England will be found in Arnold Bennett and J. B. Priestley.   Sheila Kaye Smith and Mary Webb have incidental references to rural Nonconformity.   Edward Thompson has attempted a full-length but one-sided and unattractive picture of North of England Methodism in *Introducing the Arnisons* (1935) and *John Arnison* (1943).

conformity—a Nonconformity which still winced under a sense of its social and political inferiority; not because it hankered after social prestige but because in the old Puritan phrase, these inequalities ' hurt its understanding '. It was a Nonconformity, too, which maintained its historic Cromwellian alliance with the masses of the people, a Nonconformity to which Christianity appeared in the light of a trumpet of liberation. Clifford was brought up amongst poor working people in the atmosphere of Chartism. . . . To the end of his days he preached the Christian Gospel as the Charter of all who are poor and oppressed and underprivileged."[6]

Born in a Derbyshire village in 1836, Clifford was at work in a lace factory when he was ten years old. When in his late teens, he was encouraged to become a local preacher, and in 1855 entered the Midland Baptist College, then at Leicester. Young and by no means well equipped, he settled in Paddington, which was to be the scene of his life work, in 1858, only four years after Spurgeon had come to London. Success, particularly among young people, came almost at once to Clifford, but he knew the slenderness of his intellectual armour and had a passion for knowledge. Within eight years he had secured from London University degrees in Arts, Science and Law. Then, with growing confidence, he flung himself into the life of his time, and was soon recognized as a leader of Nonconformity—a leader sympathetic with the new knowledge, one with an indignant consciousness of social and moral iniquities, a fighter of courage and resource, yet one without bitterness or guile. He was President of the Baptist Union in 1888, that is, in the midst of the " Downgrade " controversy which took Spurgeon out of the Union. A few years later he was one of the leading figures in the organization of the Free Church

[6] Jeffs, op. cit., p. 188.

Council. During the Education controversy in the next decade he was the acknowledged head of the Nonconformist forces, the life and soul of the passive resistance movement. The position he had attained was indeed a unique one, as was shown by the national testimonial given him in 1906 for his seventieth birthday. Yet his work was far from done. He continued an active crusader for many good causes, an influential leader in the Brotherhood Movement (which was one of the characteristic organizations of the time), winning the respect and affection of ever-widening circles and gaining an unusual moral authority in public affairs. There was general satisfaction when, in 1921, the King made him a Companion of Honour, the first Free Church minister to receive that high distinction. A few years earlier the Prime Minister (Mr. Lloyd George) had said: "There is no man in England upon whose conscience I would sooner ring a coin than John Clifford's." The last years of the ever-youthful veteran were given to earnest pleas, through the Free Church Council and other channels, for personal evangelism. He had passed his eighty-seventh birthday, but was still active when, in 1923, he suddenly passed away at a meeting of the Baptist Union Council.

Silvester Horne was a Liberal M.P. Throughout his long public life, John Clifford was a keen, but discriminating Liberal, with strong radical sympathies born of his knowledge and love of the working classes. As early as 1886 he was identified with a " Christian Socialist League ", and, almost alone among the prominent leaders of Nonconformity, he watched with sympathy the rise of the Labour Party. In the troubled years which followed 1918 he was even ready to support Labour Party candidates, and wrote with characteristic optimism in the year before his death: " It is clear that political thought is gravitating more and more towards the application of Christian ideas and ideals

to the life of the common people. That is the inner meaning
of the great ' Labour ' vote: and all progressive men will be
interested in the process."[7] The growth of the Labour
movement, its separation from the Liberalism which had
long been its nurse, and the subsequently chequered career
of the Liberal Party, had all a significant bearing on the
fortunes of the Free Churches.

The close connection between working-class Nonconformity and the beginnings of Trade Unionism has already
been noted. The earliest working-class M.P.s were most of
them Free Churchmen. At the very time, however, that the
workers became increasingly class-conscious and determined
on the redress of their wrongs, the Nonconformist bodies
achieved victory in their own struggle for religious equality
and became respectable and prosperous. It is difficult not
to trace a connection between, on the one hand, the new
social opportunities that came to Free Churchmen and the
increasing funds at their disposal, and, on the other, a
gradual alienation from the working classes, though there
were clearly many other causes at work as well. For a time
Nonconformity continued to give the new movement some
of the finest of its leaders. Keir Hardie, who founded the
Independent Labour Party in 1893, the year after he entered
the House of Commons, had had links with the Evangelical
Union in Scotland and was an earnest Christian man.
Arthur Henderson, whose organizing ability was largely
responsible for the increasing power of the Labour movement, and whose gifts and integrity carried him to the
highest places in the State, was a loyal Methodist and
remained throughout his life closely identified with the
Brotherhood Movement. Others might be named. Nevertheless, the early decades of the century saw the growth of
a Labour leadership often indifferent to religion or even

[7] Marchant, *op. cit.*, p. 267.

hostile, and at the same time a decline in the effectiveness of Nonconformist work in the great centres of population, and a suspicion of left-wing politics.

In not a few chapels forward-looking thinking on political, social and international matters has been looked at askance, and there have even been cases of the " persecution " and " excommunication " of those who have been too radical. In other words, during the past half century the Nonconformist churches have ceased to be identified, as they were during the previous hundred years, with the legitimate aspirations of the poor. Asked once about the decay of the religious idealism of the early Labour Party, Ramsay Macdonald replied: " You refer to a lack of a steady ethical note in our party. But that is just the complaint that so many of our people make about organized religion itself! "[8] The " Nonconformist Conscience " had indeed its last flaming apostle in John Clifford, and even in his last years it had come to be associated chiefly with total abstinence, Sunday observance, and anti-gambling agitations, all of them desirable, but hardly the most crying matters for reform in a crumbling civilization![9]

The 1914-18 war was a shattering spiritual experience, not least for those who had been brought up to believe in progress and in freedom broadening down " from precedent to precedent ", and who had thought that Jerusalem was soon to be built in England's green and pleasant land. With the war came the Russian Revolution, " the most colossal event in history since the Reformation ".[10] The miracles of wire-

[8] Arthur Porritt, *More and More Memories,* 1947, p. 131.
[9] On the matters raised in the preceding paragraph see the important *Christian News-Letter Supplement*, No. 92 (July 30th, 1941), by W. G. Symons, " Ecumenical Christianity and the Working Classes ", and two supplementary ones, No. 100 (September 24th, 1941) and No. 134 (May 20th, 1942).
[10] H. J. Laski, *Reflections on the Revolution of our Time,* 1943.

less-telegraphy and broadcasting were soon transforming human life. And at the same time knowledge of the vast world opened up by modern science began to percolate into all sections of the population. The relevance of the old phrases to the new conditions was not obvious. In the period between the wars large numbers of the population were admittedly at sea intellectually and religiously. All the churches found themselves with fewer worshippers and lost much of their authority in public life.

Nonconformity still produced notable preachers, though they were fewer than in the previous century. Preachers like F. B. Meyer, Dinsdale Young and Campbell Morgan seemed to belong to an age that had passed rather than the immediate present. More obviously products of their times were R. J. Campbell, of the City Temple, who, after repudiating the humanistic " New Theology " of his earlier years, passed into the Anglican Church, and W. E. Orchard, of the King's Weigh House, the leader of a Free Catholic Movement, who himself joined the Roman Church in 1932. Though both had large congregations, their example was followed by only a handful of others. The steadier stream of central Nonconformity was better represented by J. H. Jowett, who exercised influential ministries in Birmingham, New York and Westminster, and by J. Scott Lidgett, a shrewd and far-seeing leader of ability and conviction, whose word carried weight on both public and ecclesiastical issues.

Jowett gave the closing months of his active life to a nation-wide campaign for international peace, in collaboration with the Archbishop of York (Dr. Lang). He believed that " if the Christian Churches, should another war occur, followed the precedent they had set themselves, in all the nations, when the war broke out in 1914, the very future of

the Church itself would be in grave danger ".[11] But Jowett
did not hold the full pacifist position. The peace issue
proved an absorbing, perplexing and often divisive one for
more than a decade, in Church as well as State, and must be
reckoned one of the main factors which contributed to the
general uncertainty.

III

This, however, is not the whole story. Misunderstanding,
the separation of former friends and associates, hesitancy
and loss of power—these have to be chronicled. But there
are other things to note as well. Partly as a result of the
abolition of religious tests at Oxford and Cambridge and the
establishment there of colleges like Mansfield, Westminster,
Cheshunt, Wesley House and Regent's Park, and partly
through the organization of the modern universities, with
which most of their other theological colleges became associated, Nonconformist scholarship reached new levels and
gained recognition in all branches of the Church. At the
same time the Free Churches came closer together than ever
before, and a new era opened in the relations between the
Free Churches and the Church of England.

It will be convenient to consider first the relationship of
the Free Churches to one another. From the early days of
the Free Church Council there were some who looked
askance at its emphasis on political interests and at the lack
of any really doctrinal or ecclesiastical basis. R. W. Dale
had refused to join the new movement. Though not an old
man, he was nearing the end of his life, and he represented
the individualism of the Victorian age.[12] The new century
had not proceeded far before a younger generation had
doubts not only as to the effectiveness but as to the rightness

[11] Arthur Porritt, *John Henry Jowett,* 1924, p. 256.
[12] A. W. W. Dale, *op. cit.,* pp. 647f.

of the methods which were being pursued. The effects of the 1914-18 war, the decline in church-going, and the overlapping and sometimes apparent competition between the Free Churches quickened their feelings. These found most effective and dramatic expression in J. H. Shakespeare, the Secretary of the Baptist Union, who in 1916, when President of the National Free Church Council, had pleaded boldly for a federation, or even closer union of the Free Churches that they might more effectively minister to their generation. His ideas were eloquently and forcefully set out in a book which achieved a very wide circulation and which occasioned much controversy, *The Churches at the Cross-roads: A Study in Christian Unity*. In 1919, in response to his challenge, the Federal Council of Evangelical Free Churches was formed.

Shakespeare[13] had already rendered outstanding service to his own denomination. After a successful ministry in Norwich, he was in 1898, at the age of forty-nine, made Secretary of the Baptist Union. In a few years he had greatly extended its scope and authority. In the words of T. R. Glover, Shakespeare "taught all Baptists to form large ideals for their church, to conceive of it as a great society, where differences of tradition should not outweigh the fact of a common faith, and where women should have their function as well as men; to realize it in its world-wide range and significance; and to live more consciously as members one of

[13] Shakespeare's dates were 1857-1928. He expressly desired, probably under the physical collapse which shrouded his last years, that there should be no official biography of him. This leaves a great gap in the material available for a study of the period. It may here be noted that, following a contemporary tendency, not a few of the Free Church figures of the time—R. F. Horton, J. D. Jones, J. C. Carlile, L. P. Jacks, P. Carnegie Simpson, J. Scott Lidgett, A. E. Garvie—wrote autobiographies. It is noticeable and regrettable, though perhaps inevitable, that they do not deal specifically with many of the issues which now seem the important ones.

another." Nevertheless, by 1916 he had come to feel that mankind had entered a new era and that the day of denominationalism was past. The various Presbyterian bodies in Scotland were already drawing closer together. The Methodist groups were beginning to consider union. In Canada, Presbyterians, Methodists and Congregationalists were at work on a scheme for a United Church. What of England? Shakespeare insisted that the evangelical Free Churches were essentially one in doctrine, that there was already a large measure of common life and witness, and that such differences as existed in polity need be no bar to immediate federation, and federation perhaps only a step or so away from organic union and a United Free Church. He had no desire for complete uniformity.

After much discussion the Federal Council of Evangelical Free Churches was established. It was on a carefully representative basis. An impressive declaratory statement of common faith and practice was drawn up, but one which excluded Unitarians. Committees were appointed to work out further the implications of federation both in polity and practice. But the movement was soon deprived of Shakespeare's own leadership, though not before it had become clear that he had gone ahead of the rank and file and had caused widespread suspicion because of his often expressed hope that the Free Churches and the Anglican Church might ultimately be brought together, for the sake of which he was himself ready to accept a modified episcopacy and even some form of re-ordination.[14] The Federal Council established itself gradually, however, and became an increasingly useful clearing-house for matters of common concern, the official as opposed to the free voice of Nonconformity. Relatively little progress has been made, however, towards the effective

[14] *The Churches at the Cross-roads*, Ch. XII. Appendix II gives the Declaratory Statement.

expression of the vision of a United Free Church, in spite of
lengthy conversations between Congregationalists and Presbyterians and Congregationalists and Baptists, and in spite
of urgent pleas by individuals. Methodist Union was
achieved in 1932, and, perhaps because of their preoccupa-
tion with all the changes it has involved, Methodists have
seemed chary of further immediate discussions or commit-
ments. On the other hand, there was growing impatience,
in widely different circles, with the existence of two bodies—
the Federal Council and the National Free Church Council
—each claiming to speak on behalf of Free Churchmen, and
in 1939, just as war broke out again, they united. The new
constitution provides for an executive of the type favoured
by the Federal Council, and for local councils and an annual
Congress after the model of the older body. It is still too
early to pass judgment on the effectiveness of this development or to suggest what may be its consequences.

There has long been much intercourse and exchange
between the denominations. The different hymn books, the
forms of worship, the combined teaching and preaching, and
the training of the ministry, have approximated ever more
closely to one another. Each body has a tradition and ethos
of its own, but to the average church member these mean
far less than they once did. Moreover, the borrowing that
goes on has extended to include the Church of England.
The works of Free Church Biblical scholars and theologians
are now read and studied far beyond the borders of their
own churches. In the years we are considering, men
like A. M. Fairbairn, J. H. Moulton, W. H. Bennett,
G. Buchanan Gray, Estlin Carpenter, John Skinner, A. S.
Peake, P. T. Forsyth, J. Vernon Bartlet, John Oman,
C. Anderson Scott, A. E. Garvie, H. Wheeler Robinson
and T. R. Glover—all of them of the Free Churches—
rendered recognized service in the realm of scholarship to

L

the whole Christian Church. Their successors include men like T. W. Manson, T. H. Robinson, H. H. Rowley, C. H. Dodd, R. Newton Flew, Vincent Taylor, H. G. Wood and others too numerous to mention.[15] These are impressive names, but they represent only one side of the account. Nonconformists have been able to give much, and what they have given has gained for them a new respect. But they have also learned much from those regarded formerly with suspicion and distrust. In matters of doctrine, history and worship, and in the practical expression of the faith, Free Churchmen have increasingly discovered what Anglican scholars and the Anglican tradition have to give, and have benefited thereby. It is against this intellectual background, as well as in the light of contemporary happenings, that the mutual approaches of the churches must be considered.

As we have seen, religious development in England in the eighteenth and nineteenth centuries deepened the gulf between the Anglican and the Free Churches. The Evangelicals found a way of bridging the chasm, but they created no permanent ecclesiastical link and their co-operative efforts were viewed with a good deal of suspicion and disapproval, particularly from the Anglican side. Nevertheless, there were always a few who cherished the dream of a comprehensive National Church, the united expression of the religious insights and loyalties of the whole community. Young Arthur (afterwards Dean) Stanley may be found in 1834 busy with a scheme to make all English Christians members of

---

[15] During the same period the Church of Scotland has supplied men like Marcus Dods, George Adam Smith, T. M. Lindsay, James Denney, H. R. Mackintosh, James Moffatt and John Baillie. For Fairbairn, the first Principal of Mansfield College, Oxford, see the *Life* by W. B. Selbie, 1914. T. R. Glover, summing up in *The Times* in 1932 the Dissent of the previous fifty years, gave it as his opinion that the impress of Fairbairn on the Free Churches was deeper and more lasting than that of Spurgeon.

the National Establishment, and arguing against the idea that unity of doctrine is essential to the idea of a Christian Church.[16] All his life the subject interested him. In 1843, at a gathering in Edinburgh to commemorate the bicentenary of the Westminster Assembly, the Scottish leader Thomas Chalmers made an eloquent plea for Christian union. His slogan was " Co-operation now, and this with a view, as soon as may be, to incorporation afterwards ", and he thought of Presbyterianism as a system which might reconcile the differences between Congregationalism and Episcopacy. The Evangelical Alliance formed in 1846 seemed to Chalmers inadequate; much closer and more constant collaboration, nationally and locally, was needed.[17] Shortly after Stanley's death in 1881, another great Victorian, James Martineau, the Unitarian, then more than eighty years old, worked out a plan for a National Church of the federal type, founded on the assumption that the different communions divided the truth among them. His plan was " Disestablishment without Disendowment ", and he embodied it in a bill which could be presented to Parliament. It awakened little response.[18]

It was not until the war of 1914-18 that there became evident in this country a general sweetening of ecclesiastical relationships. It was the result partly of the increased knowledge of one another and the mutual borrowing to which allusion has already been made, partly to a world-wide movement, which will later concern us, the main inspiration of which was missionary co-operation overseas, and partly to the experiences of the war years. Individual Anglican leaders—Bishop Hensley Henson was one of the best known

[16] R. E. Prothero, *Life and Correspondence of A. P. Stanley*, 1894, I, p. 107.

[17] Hanna, *Memoirs of Dr. Chalmers*, 1852, IV, Ch. XX; Hugh Watt, *Thomas Chalmers and the Disruption*, 1943, pp. 334f.

[18] J. Estlin Carpenter, *James Martineau*, 1905, pp. 515f.

—often risking much disapproval from their own communion, showed themselves ready on occasion to enter Free Church pulpits. Nonconformists were invited to share in united services of various kinds. The post-war generation was as impatient of ecclesiastical divisions as it was ignorant of their origin and meaning. These things were the background to the historic " Appeal to all Christian People " issued in 1920 by the Anglican bishops then meeting at Lambeth, and to the discussions which followed upon it.

The bishops were gathered from all over the world and they were thinking in world terms. By the Enabling Act of 1919 the Church of England felt itself to have obtained a measure of freedom from State control, which it had not formerly had. The bishops declared that they acknowledged " all those who believe in our Lord Jesus Christ, and have been baptized into the name of the Holy Trinity, as sharing . . . membership in the universal Church of Christ which is His Body ", and pleaded for new and adventurous attempts to express visibly the fellowship of all Christian people. Non-episcopal ministries were expressly acknowledged as having been " manifestly blessed and owned by the Holy Spirit as effective means of Grace ". On the basis of an acceptance of the Bible and the Nicene Creed, the two sacraments and a ministry, universally acknowledged by means of an episcopate " exercised in a representative and constitutional manner ", the bishops believed that a united Church might be established. Their appeal met with a widespread response from the Free Churches, already prepared for such a step by the work of men like J. H. Shakespeare, although it was clear that the Quakers and the Salvation Army, as well as the Unitarians,[19] would be un-

[19] Unitarians became an organized denomination in 1928. Having close relationships with certain churches on the Continent, they shared in the " Life and Work " movement and so have a part in

able to take part in conversations on the suggested basis. Negotiations went on for several years, but made little more progress than did Richard Baxter's schemes in 1688, or the comprehension proposals of a generation later. It soon became evident that certain of the leaders were inclined for compromises that would be unacceptable to the rank and file of their communions, and this on both sides, and that there are still deep divergences of judgment as to the church polity implied by the gospel itself. Moreover, the Anglican bishops were engaged not only in discussions with English Free Churchmen, but also with the development of their own relationships with the Eastern Orthodox Churches and the Lutheran Churches, while certain individuals among them were interested in informal conversations with Roman Catholic dignitaries. The controversy which led to the rejection by Parliament of the Revised Book of Common Prayer in 1928 showed the continued strength of Protestant feeling in England. The subsequent authorization of the Book by the bishops gravely disturbed many of the Free Church leaders most eager for closer ecclesiastical fellowship.[20]

Twenty years of sporadic discussion by the Free Churches among themselves, and between Free Churchmen and Anglicans, yielded little substantial progress towards the uniting in one organization of the various Christian bodies in this country.[21] On the other hand they deepened mutual knowledge and respect. All the time practical co-operation in a

the British Council of the Churches. An invitation to Dr. L. P. Jacks to preach in Liverpool Cathedral in 1933 caused considerable outcry. Unitarians are not included in the Free Church Federal Council or in the World Council of Churches.

[20] See, e.g., P. Carnegie Simpson, *Recollections*, 1943, pp. 89f., and his comment, " Really, this was hardly cricket."

[21] See G. K. A. Bell, *Documents on Christian Unity*, first series 1924, second series 1930, third series 1948; Hugh Martin, *Christian Reunion*, 1941; *A Christian Year Book*, 1950 edition, pp. 84-107.

wide variety of enterprises was on the increase. There was to be found not only at ecclesiastical headquarters but also in town and village a spirit very different from that of the nineteenth century. Public occasions like the Coronation of George VI and National Days of Prayer brought together religious leaders in a way unknown since Commonwealth times. Broadcast services played a notable part in the surmounting of ecclesiastical barriers. Finally, the attacks upon religion on the Continent of Europe, and the notable resistance offered by Protestants, Roman Catholics and the Orthodox—drew forth a general sympathy which was one of the main factors making possible in this country " joint action in the social and parallel action in the religious field " by Free Churchmen, Anglicans and Roman Catholics. This was one of the most notable developments, religiously, during the war of 1939-45. Another important landmark was the agreement on the vexed question of religious instruction in schools which found embodiment in the Education Act of 1944.

IV

It has already been made clear that recent decades have set the ecclesiastical situation in this country in a world framework, giving it a far wider reference than a merely national one. Both the Free Churches and the Church of England are now communions of ecumenical range. The greatly improved relationships in this country have come in considerable measure from the opening up of world horizons and from the impetus of what is usually described as " the Ecumenical Movement ", which in turn has been largely the product of the striking missionary experience of the Church during the past hundred and fifty years.

One of the most significant gatherings in Christian history was the World Missionary Conference held at Edinburgh in 1910. It greatly quickened missionary enthusiasm and led, in the face of the immense tasks before Christians overseas, to the development of co-operation in planning and strategy as well as to united action in particular enterprises. It also inspired the " Life and Work " movement, which drew together Christians from all parts of the world in search of a more effective application of their message to the contemporary situation, and the " Faith and Order " movement which began to wrestle with theological and ecclesiastical divisions. Simply to name the three series of world conferences is to indicate the growing strength and influence of inter-church collaboration and fellowship. Edinburgh (1910), Jerusalem (1928) and Madras (1938) represent the development of missionary co-operation and have associated with them the National Christian Councils of many different regions overseas and the International Missionary Council. Stockholm (1925) and Oxford (1937) came out of the " Life and Work " movement. Lausanne (1927) and Edinburgh (1937) were concerned with " Faith and Order ". All three streams converged again in the Youth Conference at Amsterdam (1939) and the World Council of Churches which was formed in Amsterdam in 1948. The British agencies through which there is a sharing in all that these conferences have stood for are the Conference of British Missionary Societies, which was constituted in 1912, and the British Council of Churches formed in 1942.

The Free Church contribution to the Ecumenical Movement has been a very important one. Many of its outstanding leaders both in England and America have been Free Churchmen. Men like J. Allen Baker and Henry Hodgkin, who were Quakers, Sir Henry Lunn and John R. Mott, the one of English Methodist stock, the other of American, A. E. Garvie, a Congregationalist, and William Paton, a Presbyterian, have been key figures, and others might be named. A little reluctance was shown at first in certain quarters, but with growing confidence Free Churchmen have given themselves to the service of the World Church, to their own great enrichment as well as that of others.

Our special concern here, however, is with the situation in England, and it must be frankly admitted that the last thirty years have seen a decline in the influence of the Free Churches. They have been badly hit by the decrease in church attendance which has been general. Their impact on society has been less than in the previous fifty years. Almost all the Free Church bodies have become more centralized—the Methodists through the movements leading to the Union of 1932—the Congregationalists and Baptists through the raising of large denominational funds and certain changes in polity such as the appointment of Moderators and Superintendents. But there has been a growing sense of frustration and friction in many quarters, a loss of confidence, an uncertainty as to the future. It showed itself in the preaching of the period, in the attenuated " modernism " which succeeded the " New Theology " of Edwardian days, in the over-excited obscurantist reaction to the new knowledge in certain quarters, in the all but exclusive emphasis on the " social gospel " in others, in the topical sermon, and kindred devices, all of them a sad decline from the great days of the Nonconformist pulpit. The Church Meeting, once one of the main centres of life among Baptists and Congregationalists, has decayed, as has the class meeting in Methodism. During the same period, moreover, there have been vigorous stirrings of life within the Church of England, and a bolder and more spiritual leadership on moral and social questions than has ever before come from within the Establishment. This, as well as less attractive considerations, contributed to the failure of Nonconformity to hold not a few of its most gifted children.

Is this decline more than temporary? Is it to be compared with what happened in the eighteenth century? Or have the Free Churches fulfilled their mission and is their day over? Who shall say? What is clear is that in quite recent days there is a renewed and deeper and more theological questioning among Free Churchmen, a more urgent prayer, a return to a study of their origins and a parallel endeavour to relate their specific message to the contemporary world.[22] This chapter, whose aim is faithful chronicling, not prophecy, should not therefore end in a minor key. What Professor E. H. Carr says of British life in general is, we may dare to believe, apposite. The life of the nation is intimately connected with that of the Free Churches. " The fact," he declares, " that there is now a widespread consciousness of the decline in British unity, initiative and determination during that period (i.e. the twenty years prior to 1939), combined with a marked revival of these qualities since 1940, provides the firmest ground of hope that this revival will not end with the war."[23] Though the cloud on the Free Church horizon be but the size of a man's hand it is assuredly there as a sign of recovery and renewal.

---

[22] The debate has been most vigorous in Congregationalism. See *Essays Congregational and Catholic* (edited by A. Peel), 1931; Albert Peel, *Inevitable Congregationalism*, 1937, and *The Christian Basis of Democracy*, 1943; N. Micklem, *Congregationalism To-day*, 1937, and *Congregationalism and the Church Catholic*, 1943; D. T. Jenkins, *The Nature of Catholicity*, 1942; *Congregationalism To-day* (edited by J. Marsh), 1943. With these more recent works may be mentioned P. T. Forsyth, *The Church and the Sacraments*, 1917; like all Forsyth's work, it has received increasing attention of late years. Note also a renewed interest in Nonconformist history and books such as G. F. Nuttall, *The Holy Spirit in Puritan Faith and Experience*, 1946, Horton Davies, *The Worship of the English Puritans*, 1948, and H. Townsend, *The Claims of the Free Churches,* 1949. See also *The Catholicity of Protestantism*, 1950, a report presented to the Archbishop of Canterbury by a group of Free Churchmen.

[23] *Conditions of Peace*, p. 130.

CHAPTER NINE

The Contribution of the Free Churches

The ideal of a free Church in a free State is not less necessary or less likely to be fruitful in the world of the present than it has been in the past. Its fruitfulness is showing itself in all kinds of new ways and opportunities.

A. D. LINDSAY,
The Church and Democracy, p. 87.

None who has left a Christianity based on authority can return to anything but a Christianity which is free.

N. BERDYAEV.

HERE, THEN, is the story of the Free Churches. Their contribution to Christendom has been rich and varied. In a few final pages there is space for only brief comments and reflections. Nonconformity, for all the disappointments and perplexities of the last thirty years, remains a very important factor in the religious life of the nation, and in a world-setting becomes of even greater significance.

An attempt was made a few years ago to study the distribution of the Free Churches in England from a sociological point of view.[1] Much that is of interest emerges. In Cornwall and Lincolnshire there are chapels in almost every parish, and in the industrial north there are hardly any

[1] Frank Tillyard, "The Distribution of the Free Churches in England", *Sociological Review*, Vol. XXVII (1935), pp. 1-18.

populated areas where the Free Churches are not represented. This is not true in the south of England, where
there are considerable districts hardly touched by Nonconformity. Taken together, however, the Free Churches have
some six thousand trained ministers in England. About
three thousand of them are Methodists. The other three
thousand are divided among the Congregationalists, Baptists
and Presbyterians in the proportion of five, four and one.
On the whole, the geographical distribution of Methodism
may be said to be complementary to that of the other bodies.
Its connexional system has had particular success both in
rural and working-class areas. The Baptist, Congregational
and Presbyterian systems, with the greater independence
they give to the local church and the greater financial responsibility resting upon it, have had their chief success in the
urban areas, save in those parts of the country where Puritanism was particularly strong in the seventeenth century.
There are nearly three hundred churches which have a
continuous history stretching back to 1662 or even earlier,
and these are mainly in London and the eastern counties or
in the south-west. Methodism achieved great success in the
evangelization of Cornwall and also in the industrial areas
of the north. Modern Presbyterianism is to be found
specially strong in the most northerly counties and around
Liverpool.

" One of the most distinctive facts about British working-
class life," wrote Mr. W. G. Symons in 1941, " has been
its roots in Nonconformist Christianity. . . . The Labour
Party, trade unions in their British form, and a great part
of British democratic thought and effort have come from
working-class nonconformity; however much they are
divorced from the life of the churches now, they still bear
upon them the marks of their origin. It is just impossible to
understand the British labour movement or co-operative

institutions without a knowledge of Methodism—but not so much the Methodism of ecclesiastical debate as the Methodism of the village chapel. . . . We have in Great Britain what is perhaps unique in Christian history—a religious tradition that is native and indigenous to an *industrial* proletariat."[2] Here again we have an estimate from a mainly sociological standpoint. We may set beside Mr. Symons's judgment, which concentrates attention on the strength of Nonconformity, particularly Methodism, in industrial areas, an interesting remark of Edwyn Bevan which suggests important historical parallels and is presumably intended to embrace the whole of Nonconformist history rather than the last century and a half. " Probably," he says, with the early Christian centuries in mind, " the Church drew the bulk of its adherents from small tradesmen and handicraftsmen, an analogy of the respectable, law-abiding class from which the Nonconformist communities in England draw most of their adherents."[3]

None of these suggestions, however, exhausts the range of the Nonconformity we have been tracing from its rise at the end of the sixteenth century and which has spread from England to the American Continent and to many other lands. Sir Ernest Barker adopts a rather different standpoint, and, as noted in our first chapter, uses the tension between the Anglican and Free Churches as the chief key to the interpretation of modern British history and to the understanding of the British character.[4] This introduces wider and deeper issues than the merely sociological approach, but it still fails to reach the spiritual sources of the movement as a whole.

We come nearer to these in the remarks of two distin-

[2] " Ecumenical Christianity and the Working Classes ", *Christian News-Letter Supplement*, No. 92. Cf. Supplements Nos. 100 and 134.
[3] *Christianity*, 1932, p. 45.
[4] *Britain and the British People*, 1942, pp. 24-6, and Ch. V, *passim*.

guished Congregationalist scholars, Dr. Fairbairn, of Oxford, and Mr. Bernard Manning, of Cambridge. " The ultimate grounds, I will not say of our Nonconformity, but of our existence as Free Churches of Jesus Christ," wrote Fairbairn, " are theological and religious, not political. Our reasons for dissenting from the Church of England are too fundamental to be merely or mainly ecclesiastical. We dissent because we believe that she fails adequately to interpret and realize for the people of England the religion of Christ."[5] " Our specific form of churchmanship," said Manning, " is at least as old as the historic Anglican Settlement. I should claim indeed that it is older, that it goes back to Geneva—to say nothing of the New Testament. Ecclesiastically, we deal with the Anglicans on equal terms."[6] And again, in words that cover Presbyterian and Baptist origins, Manning wrote : " Congregationalism came into being as the result of the working of three historical forces. It is a mixture composed of three main ingredients : the historic deposit of the holy, apostolic, evangelical, catholic faith, the new apprehension of that faith which came to Western Europe in the sixteenth century, and certain ecclesiastical arrangements made in England in the sixteenth and seventeenth centuries."[7]

Even these judgments may to-day be charged with concentrating attention exclusively upon the Free Church tradition as an English religious phenomenon, but they clearly take us nearer to the heart of the matter.

II

" No movement as fruitful as English Nonconformity ever nourished itself mainly on negations," said Bernard

[5] *Studies in Religion and Theology*, 1910, p. 5.
[6] *Essays in Orthodox Dissent*, 1939, p. 145.
[7] *Ibid.*, p. 158.

Manning.[8] Is it possible briefly to sum up the main characteristics and chief emphases of the type of religion with
which we have been concerned? What are the truths upon
which it has ventured? "The Nonconformist spirit," says
H. W. Clark, " is, in succinct summary, the spirit which
exalts life above organization. More than that, it is the
spirit which holds that life should *make* organization."[9]
The principle herein enshrined constitutes, he believes, a
crucial dividing-line in the interpretation of the Christian
faith. Free Churchmen, throughout their history, wherever
they have been true to themselves, have insisted on the
primacy of the gospel over all matters of church polity and
organization. First comes faith, then order. They have not
believed that the gospel of Jesus Christ is bound up with any
particular ecclesiastical structure, or was committed to any
hierarchical or priestly succession. There have been times
when this spiritual principle has been obscured. It has
implications which each generation—and not least our own
—must work out for itself. We may, however, accept it as
our starting-point and go on to note certain consequences
which have followed from it.

First, Nonconformists have insisted on the necessity of
personal decision regarding God's offer of salvation to men.
We are not born Christians, nor can we be made Christians
by others, not even by the Church. God has given us freedom, and salvation is by faith, personal faith. The reverse
side of this is a belief in what an American Baptist thinker

[8] *The Making of Modern English Religion*, p. 104.
[9] *Op. cit.*, I, p. 3. Cf. Shillito, *op. cit.*, p. 16: "The life must
determine the form." For an interpretation of the history of the
early Christian centuries from this standpoint see J. Vernon Bartlet,
Church-Life and Church-Order (Birkbeck Lectures, 1924), 1943.
That some Anglicans would accept the supremacy of faith over order
may be seen from C. S. Carter, *The Reformation and Reunion*, 1935.
A sharply contrasted standpoint will be found in the writings of
K. E. Kirk, A. G. Hebert and A. M. Ramsey.

called " the competence of the soul in matters of religion ",[10] and what R. W. Dale had in mind when he linked " the spiritual root of Independency " with " the ultimate secret of Puritanism ", defining their purpose as " to assert and vindicate the reality, the greatness, the completeness of the redemption that is in Christ, and the nearness of God to the soul of man ".[11] This has resulted at its best in a noble Christian individualism. The dignity and value of the individual soul have been asserted and defended in opposition to those who would place the group or the Church in a position of authority. What Sir Ernest Barker says of the seventeenth-century Puritan has been true of the Nonconformist generally. " He might serve the chosen people, and through the chosen people he might serve the nation; but the service of which he always thought was the ultimate and lonely service which he owed directly to God."[12]

Secondly, there has grown from this the belief in the Church as a company of believers, a regenerate " gathered " community, a fellowship of men and women who are consciously and deliberately endeavouring " to learn all they can and practise all they know of the will of Jesus Christ ", a company of which Christ Himself is the head. " Only those who are in Christ have any right to be in the Church," said Dale,[13] and what he said with Congregationalism in mind has also been the ideal of the other Free Churches. But, " where the Spirit of the Lord is, there is liberty " (2 Corinthians iii. 17), and this has been interpreted as meaning freedom of inspiration, freedom from set and uniform liturgical forms in worship, freedom from the imposition of binding credal formularies, freedom from any confining of the grace of God to a particular form of church

[10] E. Y. Mullins.   [11] *Essays and Addresses,* 1899, pp. 250-1.
[12] *Oliver Cromwell,* p. 85.   [13] *Op. cit.,* p. 123, cf. p. 185.

order, to a priestly succession, or even to the channels of the sacraments, sacred as they are generally held to be. The liberty of the Christian man has meant liberty of conscience. The liberty of the Church has meant an assertion of " the Crown Rights of the Redeemer "[14] against any claims to authority over it by the State. Here Presbyterian, Congregationalist, Baptist, Quaker and Methodist have all been at one.

Thirdly, this belief in the freedom of the Church under the guidance of the Spirit has led to an emphasis on " the priesthood of all believers ". It has been generally agreed that certain individuals should be called out from the Church and set aside to be ministers of the Word and the Sacraments, but they are not regarded as a priestly caste or order, able to transmit from one to another any special " grace ". The Free Churches have constantly insisted on the responsibilities of all the church members, and have been ready to make the fullest use of the leadership of " lay " men. Women also have been given a freedom and opportunity not granted in other traditions. There is to be linked with this the emphasis on preaching—on the proclamation of the gospel—and on evangelism—the constant and sustained attempt, shared in by all believers, to spread the knowledge of the gospel by every means in their power.

Fourthly, there has resulted a constant endeavour to relate religion to life. Nonconformity has stressed personal conduct and the application of Christian principles to everyday affairs and to the life of society. Religion has not been regarded as a matter of special days or sacred rites so much as doing justly, loving mercy and walking humbly with God.

[14] Cf. J. S. Whale, *The Crown Rights of the Redeemer*, an Address delivered on May 17th, 1934, and P. Carnegie Simpson, *Life of Rainy*, II, Ch. xxvii.

The Free Churches can, of course, claim no monopoly of these characteristics, and on the very matters that they have thought their peculiar concern have much to learn from others. Baron von Hügel in a frank and penetrating essay on "The Convictions common to Catholicism and Protestantism", singled out for commendation three truths insisted on by Protestant Nonconformists—(1) that Religion is a Work of Man—a deliberate, lifelong, methodical renunciation and self-discipline; (2) that Man even in his present earthly condition can, through God's grace, attain in this work on himself to a Real, not an imputed, Sanctity; and (3) that the Church is Free—the visible Society of Believers, distinct from and independent of the State. All three of these truths he claimed to find in Catholicism.[15] At different times and in different communities now one and now another of the points to which we have drawn attention has had special prominence given to it. The Free Churches have never fully lived up to or expressed their own deepest convictions, but they are not alone in that. "The failure of a society to live up to an ideal does not invalidate the ideal."[16] What has been set out in the preceding paragraphs would appear to be the distinguishing marks of the Nonconformist tradition, characteristically its own when they are brought together under the inspiration of the main principle of the subordination of all organization to the spiritual life. It is only such a religious interpretation that is adequate to account not only for the Free Church tradition in England, but for its strength in America and other lands to which it has spread of recent generations. A historian looking back from the end of the present century

[15] *Essays and Addresses*, First Series, 1921, No. 9.
[16] Nevins and Commager, *America, The Story of a Free People*, p. 87. Cf. R. W. Dale, *Essays and Addresses,* p. 215: "Congregationalism, as conceived by its founders, was an ideal polity."

M

may indeed discover the most significant contemporary Free
Church movements to have been those on the continent of
Europe and in South America.

III

There are, however, certain admissions to be made at this
point. There have been tensions within Nonconformity
which cannot be ignored if its history and its present position are rightly to be understood. There have been serious
limitations in its outlook. Further, its historic witness has
not passed unregarded. Those of other traditions have
manifestly learned from it.

Nonconformity is not homogeneous, either historically or
theologically, either in practice or in theory. The first point
is made clear by the story we have unfolded. Many streams
have contributed to the broad flood of Free Church witness.
Puritans and Separatists, Congregationalists and Baptists,
Quakers, Independents and Presbyterians, Methodists and
Unitarians—all of these, and other groups, fall under the
general designation of Free Churchmen, and there are many
matters on which they hold very different views. Whether
the differences are really any greater than those, say, of the
various parties within the Anglican Church, may be doubt-
ful; but dissenting Anglicans are held together in one visible
organization—by its State establishment some would say, by
its episcopate others urge—whereas the Free Church bodies
have only recently sought more than the comradely relations
of those facing in the same general direction and seeking the
redress of common grievances. That there are deeper agree-
ments and interconnections their history makes clear, but it
is only in the last half century—it might be said, only since
1919—that closer federation and unity have been sought.

"Dissidence"—to use Burke's word—is perhaps a necessary accompaniment of Dissent, if the spiritual principle on

which it rests be understood. It is likely and right that there should be differences of belief and practice among Christians. This is part of the price which must be paid for freedom. If, however, that freedom be truly a part of the gospel itself, then it is a price paid by God as well as man, and it will be discovered to be less heavy and dangerous than that involved in uniformity or submission to authority. Some words of John Milton are still relevant: " What some lament of, we rather should rejoice at, should rather praise this pious forwardness among men, to reassume the ill-reputed care of their Religion into their own hands again. A little generous prudence, a little forbearance of one another, and some grain of charity might win all these diligences to join, and unite in one general and brotherly search of the Truth."[17]

Discussions about Free Church unity have inevitably uncovered differences in regard to the theory of the Church. The long shadow of 1662 still lies across the older Nonconformist bodies. Not a few of those standing in the succession of the Independents and of those Presbyterians who, in the eighteenth century, became one with them, are Nonconformists not of choice but of necessity. They would gladly join a comprehensive National Church were the Act of Uniformity repealed and were there adequate safeguards against Erastianism. They are not averse to a National Church as such and would be ready for considerable sacrifices to secure the union of English Christians in one visible fellowship. The conflicts of the twentieth century have brought a number of Nonconformists to believe that " perhaps there is some value, after all, in the public acknowledgment of Christ's claim over the national life ".[18]

[17] *Areopagitica*, 1644.
[18] H. F. Lovell Cocks, *The Nonconformist Conscience*, 1943, p. 93. The context provides a good illustration of this more sympathetic

Many Methodists share this general standpoint. On the other hand, to-day, as in the seventeenth century, a large number of Free Churchmen reject any conception which links together Church and State, or Church and Nation. "Such a view", they would say—borrowing the language of a distinguished Anglican scholar, noting the number of Anglicans who have come to question the value and rightness of establishment, and finding confirmation in recent happenings on the continent of Europe—"Such a view is worse than a corruption of Christianity; it is a denial of the very essence of the Church, of the character which it had from the beginning as a society in which membership represented a personal individual act of will: it is an assimilation of Christianity to the State religions of paganism."[19]

Further, there are theological divergences among Free Churchmen. From Reformation times comes the broad distinction between Calvinists and Arminians, and this sometimes showed itself—as in the case of the Baptists—within one denomination. The issue ceased to be divisive in the nineteenth century, though it has to some extent been revived under the influence of the Neo-Calvinism of Karl Barth. The legacy of the eighteenth century was a tension as to the authority of the ancient creeds of the Church. The Unitarian body arose out of the controversy over subscription to creeds and formularies, which created also within the older bodies a left and right wing. Left-wing tendencies became particularly noticeable within Congregationalism, and this movement was reinforced by the controversies over

attitude to the establishment. It may be compared with T. S. Eliot, *The Idea of a Christian Society*, 1939—the work of an Anglican, whose family long had had Unitarian affiliations.

[19] Edwyn Bevan, *Christianity in the Light of Modern Knowledge*, 1929, p. 104. Cf. Bevan, *The Christian Faith*, 1936, p. 246.

evolution and Biblical criticism.[20] On the whole, during the last century and a half, the Baptists have shown themselves theologically conservative. Some ascribe this to their practice of believers' baptism, but it has to be admitted that, in the seventeenth and eighteenth centuries, Baptists were by no means among the most orthodox. Moreover, the rite of baptism has itself proved an acute difficulty in the way of the closer union of the various Free Church bodies. There is to-day less readiness than there was in the seventeenth and eighteenth centuries to join in one Christian fellowship those upholding believers' baptism and those who baptize infants. These and other differences complicate the discussions between the various bodies, and do so the more since the latter are now world-wide in extent and the divergent tendencies are most of them reproduced overseas.

We pass on to note certain obvious limitations in the Free Church outlook and tradition as it has expressed itself in the last three hundred and fifty years. Dr. Inge was once tempted into quoting with apparent approval—it was in 1908 —the remark of a seventeenth-century divine about " the meretricious gaudiness of the Church of Rome and the squalid sluttery of fanatic conventicles ".[21] What has been recalled in these pages should have shown how far from the truth such offensive words are. It may be confessed, however, that the Free Churches have not made any great

[20] For a contemporary statement of the issues see N. Micklem, *What is the Faith?*, 1936, and C. J. Cadoux, *The Case for Evangelical Modernism*, 1938.

[21] *Outspoken Essays*, I, 1919, p. 107. An even more unfortunate remark is that of Hensley Henson, *The Church of England*, 1939, p. 238: " The Dissenters are handicapped by the weakness of their systems, the crudity of their distinctive beliefs and the repulsiveness of their ' corybantic ' methods." On p. 250 he admits that at the present time the ordained ministers of the Free Churches are not inferior, socially or intellectually, to the Anglican clergy.

contribution to literature or the arts.[22] So far as Science is concerned the tradition of their academies and colleges should preserve them from reproach. Æsthetic considerations, both in architecture and in worship, have been largely ignored, partly of necessity, for during most of their history they have had few resources or opportunities for busying themselves with such matters, but mainly—and this is the point—because they were giving their attention deliberately to things regarded as more important, because, in a word, the moral categories seemed to them a surer and safer channel to the divine than the æsthetic ones. There has often been, unfortunately, ethical narrowness and a concentration on minor matters. The local churches have sometimes been " little gardens walled around ", and the liberty and equality claimed have been for the saints alone. There has been an excessive individualism. Liberty has degenerated into licence. The churches have meant more than the Church, Holy, Catholic and Apostolic. But why go on? Are these faults not to be found elsewhere? And are they not in large measure the inevitable price which frail human beings must pay for such positive insights and achievements as are theirs?

It is more important to note how the witness of the Free Churches has at many points caused substantial modification in the outlook and practice of the Church of England. Glaring abuses and anomalies have gradually been righted. An evangelical tradition, a Christian socialist party, a Life and Liberty movement have all sprung up within Anglicanism. A Church Assembly, Provincial Conferences and Parochial Church Councils are now functioning within the

[22] W. J. Turner, *English Music* (Britain in Pictures Series), 1943, p. 31, suggests that the musical decline in the eighteenth and nineteenth centuries was largely due to the religious division of the people in England. On the charge in general see Scholes, *Puritans and Music in England and New England,* 1934.

Anglican Church. As successor to Laud, there has been an Archbishop who was looked to for spiritual and moral leadership by Free Churchmen as well as by those of his own communion. It was Dr. Temple, who many years ago wrote: "As a rule, men are right when they assert and wrong when they deny. Those who have insisted on the value of liturgical worship are right; so are those who have insisted on the value of *ex tempore* and open congregational prayer. Those who have insisted on a ministry of order are right; and so are those who have insisted that the wind bloweth where it listeth, and the spirit of prophecy may light on any man."[23]

IV

What, then, of the present situation? What of the future? Certain things seem clear, though they can be set down here only in the baldest terms.

1. The study of Christian origins and of Christian history —conducted with great intensity by the scholarship of recent generations—has not invalidated the basic Free Church contention that Faith comes before Order, the Gospel before the Church. Tradition, whether in doctrine or practice, is a valuable guide but a poor master. The Free Churches have much to learn from other Christian communions, but their central principle has been vindicated again and again in history. It is impossible in the twentieth century to put back the wine of the Spirit into the old bottles of ecclesiastical order, or to assert that any one kind of polity, even episcopacy, is essential to the life and unity of the Church.

2. The contemporary situation emphasizes the responsibility of Free Churchmen for the truths they have stressed. It is not fanciful to connect the failure of political democracy on the Continent with the absence there of a sturdy religious

[23] *Foundations*, 1912, p. 355.

tradition of the Free Church type. How different the history of Europe might have been had the Reformation been carried through more radically in Germany and the neighbouring lands! It would have created individuals with a better understanding of freedom and tolerance. The deep cleavage between Church and Community, which has been so noticeable a feature of continental life in recent generations, might have been avoided. A working-class leadership, religious in outlook and temper, might have emerged. The issue of Church and State would have been faced long ago. Similarly, how different Russian history might have been had Free Church witness reached that land a hundred or even fifty years earlier than it did! Even England still needs the kind of emphasis which has been characteristic of Nonconformity. "Toleration is not a state or a theory which, once achieved, endures for ever like some principle of human knowledge. It is a principle which each generation has to strive for afresh, in theory as in practice, because even when secured it remains the most precarious of all human achievements."[24] Further, the type of character produced by Nonconformity at its best is sorely needed in the present generation.

3. Though there is much to make us rejoice in the broader attitude and spirit now shown by the Church of England, there is as yet no satisfying evidence that the National Church, as it at present exists, or as it is likely to be in the immediate future, will adequately express or safeguard the essential emphases of the Free Churches. It is difficult to see how a church which is State established and which regards episcopal government and liturgical services as essential to its life can give sufficient freedom to comprehend within itself the spontaneous, vigorous and varied expres-

[24] T. Lyon, *The Theory of Religious Liberty in England, 1603-39*, 1937, p. 232.

sions of the gospel which have been created by the Free Church tradition. The difficulties which beset the scheme for a United Church in South India are slight compared with those which have to be surmounted in this country before organic union between Anglicans and Free Churchmen is possible.

4. All our living and thinking must in future be done in " global " terms. The Free Church bodies have no longer to think of themselves as simply *vis-à-vis* the established Church of England. The past thirty years may have been disturbing and disheartening here in this country, but the Free Churches are now both severally and jointly world-wide in range. We can no longer consider a merely national settlement of religious issues. " The problem of home re-union," says Dr. Henson, " has to be considered in a new setting. It has acquired an Ecumenical setting."[25] Free Churchmen—as well as Anglicans—have responsibilities to those of their own faith and order overseas. The full effect of this on ecclesiastical matters is not yet revealed to us, but it is at least clear—and again, both to Anglicans and Free Churchmen—that, in attempting to remedy one separation, we must be cautious lest others are created.

5. It is clearer to Christian people to-day than at any previous period in Christian history that the followers of Jesus Christ should be in the closest possible fellowship with one another. This has been a deepening conviction now for several decades in all branches of the Christian Church. A world divided by racial, national and economic antagonisms looks wistfully to Christians to show it the path to unity, and to give it power to walk along that path. But, already, apart from this, Christians have felt resting upon them the eyes of the One Who prayed for His disciples " that they may all be one; even as Thou, Father, art in Me, and I in Thee,

[25] *The Church of England,* 1939, p. 251.

that they also may be in Us: that the world may believe that Thou didst send Me." (John xvii. 21.) However ancient and deep-seated the divisions, both theoretical and practical, they cannot be accepted as final by one who ponders those words. The way to unity, however, cannot be by the sacrifice of truth or principle, or by the repudiation of the spiritual heritage of any branch of the Church.

6. " The old world is dead. The future lies with those who can resolutely turn their back on it and face the new world with understanding, courage and imagination."[26] We cannot yet see very far ahead in right relationships with other Christian bodies. We cannot yet see clearly how the Church is to play its part either within the nation, or between the nations, or in the midst of vast new economic forces. Men and nations cry out for spiritual renewal. But the future alone can show whether, if and when revival comes, it will give new life to the Free Churches as they are at present organized, whether it will revive the classic modes of worship and polity associated with the Free Church tradition, or whether—from among those of every branch of the Church who are " on the outlook for the reign of God "—the Spirit will have once again to shape its own forms according to new patterns, or rather, according to those heavenly patterns of which all our ecclesiastical phrases and practices are but faulty human expressions. This the future only can show. But " whatever may be said against Dissent, it presupposes—or should presuppose—the quality of courage ".[27] The true Free Churchman has never been afraid of new situations. He has believed in the resources and guidance of the living Spirit of God, and since he has thought of church order and organization as secondary, has been able to adapt them to changing circumstances and has

[26] E. H. Carr, *Conditions of Peace*, p. 275.
[27] Sir Arthur Quiller-Couch, *Hetty Wesley*, Preface to 1908 edition.

learned by his experiments. His over-riding concern has been to make known the gospel.

7. Certain immediate tasks, therefore, face Free Churchmen. First, they must work out, more adequately and effectively than has so far been done, what is involved in membership of the Free Church Federal Council, the British Council of Churches and the World Council of Churches. Secondly, they must renew their own life by hard thinking about theological issues, particularly those connected with the doctrine of the Church. Thirdly, they must determine the relationship of their beliefs and polity to the modern economic situation and to the kind of planned society that is now evolving. Fourthly, they must recover their evangelistic zeal, that is, their sense of conviction and mission in the service of the gospel and must express their message in terms that meet the needs of man in the twentieth century.

Who that considers the story that has here been told dare assert that the work of the Free Churches, either here or in other parts of the world, is accomplished? " I am verily persuaded," said John Robinson, " that the Lord has more Truth yet to break forth out of His holy Word." He was speaking to a gallant little company who, venturing into the unknown in loyalty to their convictions, discovered a New World.

Index

188